Meeting with Danger

I could barely see two dark spots far in the distance, but all of a sudden my curls felt as if they wanted to stand straight up. My heart started hammering so hard I could feel it in my ears. Could it be . . . ?

I continued to watch, but the shapes didn't fade or keep moving ahead of us as the mirage did. They became larger and seemed to multiply as we got closer. First it looked like two people, then four, then more. They appeared to be on horses. I grabbed Papa's arm.

"Oh-oh," Papa said.

"Oh-oh, what?" Ed asked him.

"You'll find out sooner than you want to," Papa warned.

"Indians!" Ed gasped, sounding scared, not excited.

Just at that moment I heard a shriek that curdled my blood.

THE OTHER SIDE OF THE DOOR

JOY N. HULME

Published by
Deseret Book Company
Salt Lake City, Utah

In loving memory of Ora D.,
who told me her story

Some of the material in *The Other Side of the Door* has appeared previously in story form in *The Friend* magazine and is used by permission of The Church of Jesus Christ of Latter-day Saints.

Library of Congress Cataloging-in-Publication Data

Hulme, Joy N.
The other side of the door / by Joy N. Hulme.
p. cm.
Summary: Nine-year-old Dora, who has been kept out of school because of her speech impediment, dreams of learning to speak normally as her family joins a group of other Mormons journeying from Utah to New Mexico in 1910.
ISBN 0-87579-412-2
[1. Speech disorders—Fiction. 2. Frontier and pioneer life—Fiction. 3. New Mexico—Fiction. 4. Mormons—Fiction.]
I. Title.
PZ7.H88450t 1990
[Fic]—dc20 90-41020
CIP
AC

Printed in the United States of America

10 9 8 7 6 5 4 3 2 1

Contents

	Map of the Trail	vi
1	Hearing the News	1
2	Wordless Messages	11
3	Everything Bad Has Some Good	21
4	Everything Good Has Some Bad	32
5	But with Joy Wend Your Way	39
6	Baby Talk	48
7	"I Love Mama"	57
8	In Indian Country	67
9	The Tormentors	75
10	Pagosa Springs	84
11	Churning the Butter	94
12	Thanksgiving	102
13	Dream or Nightmare?	108
14	Only God Knows	119
15	Christmas in New Mexico	127
16	Another Secret	136
17	The Singing Spring	149
18	The Other Side	160
	About the Author	169

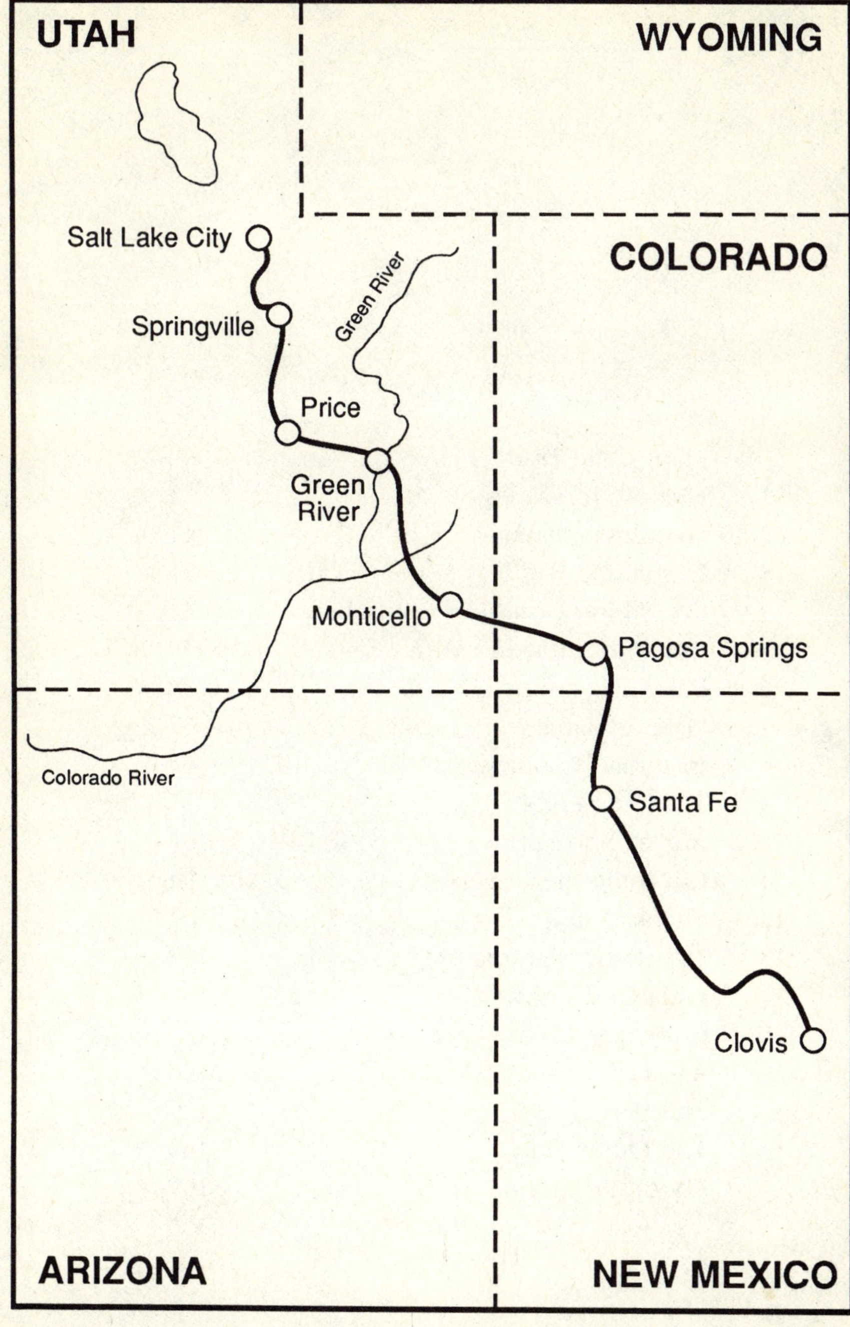
UTAH
WYOMING
COLORADO
ARIZONA
NEW MEXICO
Salt Lake City
Springville
Green River
Price
Green
River
Monticello
Pagosa Springs
Colorado River
Santa Fe
Clovis

Chapter 1

Hearing the News

It's awful to be the first one to know the good news and not be able to tell it.

When I heard Papa talking to Mama that sunny September morning in 1910, I got so excited that I wanted to let Caroline, Ed, and everyone else know what was going to happen. But telling people things was something I couldn't do.

No matter how hard I tried to make the ideas come out crisp and clear the way I was thinking them, my tongue didn't work right. Every time I opened my mouth to talk, the words were all mixed up and mushy and sounded more like grunts and groans than speaking.

I could usually get what I wanted by nudging the person next to me, making a growly noise, and pointing to the thing I needed. I could say yes or no by nodding or shaking my head, but explaining anything was almost impossible. Sometimes I tried to draw pictures or act things out to make them clear, but there are some words that just have to be spoken or else the message gets all mixed up.

My brother Ed was my special friend, and he tried to make sense out of the different signals I gave him. I could usually get him to understand what I meant—but not always. And it took so long. Papa and Mama could tell a lot about how I felt from the look on my face. But most people either made fun of me, or they pretended I wasn't there at all. It seemed easier to keep my mouth shut, so most of the time I did, unless it was about something really important. Then, if no one could understand me, the feelings inside me got so swollen up and tight that I almost exploded and I had to let them out some way.

Because I couldn't talk, I was considered stupid and wasn't allowed to attend school. I should have been going into fourth grade because I was like the middle of a sandwich between Caroline, who was in fifth, and Ed, in third. Even Frank had started school and was learning to read.

Since Papa's initials were A. B. C., for Albert B. Cookson, and Mama's name, Betty, began with the second letter, they decided to go on down the alphabet when they named their children. So far they had two girls: Caroline and me (Dora), and four boys: Ed, Frank, George, and baby Howie.

"Only eighteen more to go, Hon," Papa liked to tease Mama, "until we get to 'Z.' "

I hated staying home from school, especially in the afternoon when the two little boys took their naps and I had to figure out something quiet to do while they were asleep. That's why I was playing house by myself under the trailing branches of the weeping willow tree when I heard Papa talking to Mama on the back porch.

As I rocked my twin handkerchief dolls in their cradle tied between two dangling branches, it was easy to tell how excited he was by the tone of his voice. Even though he was trying not to disturb the napping babies, his words were coming out louder and louder and faster and faster. I moved quietly to the bottom step to listen.

"Our prayers are going to be answered at last!" Papa exclaimed. "We'll finally have a place of our own. Just think, Hon, *our own* farm! Our golden opportunity!" Papa grabbed her in a tight hug.

After a minute he went on. "We've known for a long time that Dad's eight acres here in Holladay couldn't stretch far enough to feed all of his children and all of their children, too. It's been plain that some of us would have to leave sooner or later. Well, now's our chance. This is the time."

Mama asked, "And just where is this Garden of Eden that you have in mind?"

"New Mexico," Papa said. "Clovis, New Mexico. There's some homestead land down there."

"Did the government open up a new section?"

"No. A few pieces are available because the previous owners defaulted."

"How'd they do that?" Mama wanted to know.

"Didn't live up to their agreements to make improvements on the land the way they were supposed to. Or else they didn't live on it enough months out of the year."

"So they lost it?"

"Yup. The government took it back, and now we have a chance to get it."

"Couldn't we lose it the same way?"

"Of course not. That only happens to someone who is shiftless and lazy. We're young and healthy and used to hard work."

"And we have six children to help us," Mama added proudly.

"A hundred and sixty acres," Papa mused, "to grow anything we want—corn, beans, potatoes, wheat . . . and plenty of *watermelons* for *dear little Dora* . . . " He raised his voice and looked in my direction to make sure I heard. I smiled back that I did.

Did he say a hundred and sixty acres of watermelons? For me? I couldn't believe my ears. Just imagine, a huge field full of my favorite fruit. Miles and miles of fat green melons all ready to cut into rosy wedges shaped like smiles. Oh, that delicious, sweet, juicy, drizzle-down-the-chin goodness that was so refreshing on a hot summer day! My mouth began to water at the very thought.

I loved to see how far I could spit the slick black watermelon seeds. Every year some volunteer plants sprouted up in the grass where we'd spit our seeds the year before, and I would point them out to Papa so he could transplant them to the vegetable garden.

He always shook his head and told me, "Can't grow melons in Holladay. They never get ripe. Frost comes too late in the spring and too early in the fall, and the nights are too cool in the summer. Now, up in Centerville, it's different. That's the place to grow watermelons."

Every summer we bought one or two melons for extra special occasions, but money was too scarce to do that very often. Mama fixed round slices cut in half, and we held them in our hands to gobble out the juicy red centers. We always ate melon outside so the juice wouldn't drip on the floor and make a sticky mess. My mouth was always watering for another slice. Would it really be possible to have all I wanted in New Mexico? For breakfast, dinner, and supper? And even two or three times in between? I couldn't believe it.

I picked up a stick and began to draw in the dirt

a whole row of smiling half-slices of watermelon, one right next to the other. The pretty scalloped pattern forming on the ground started an idea itching in the back of my mind. I needed a design for something. What was it? Before I figured it out, I heard Mama asking about the school.

"Don't worry," Papa assured her, "there will be a school. Close enough to walk to, I'll bet."

I hoped they'd let me go to school in New Mexico. No one knew how much I wanted to go. I was sure that, when I learned how to read and write and spell, it would be like talking because then I could put my thoughts on paper. But since I couldn't talk, everyone thought I was dumb. So I wasn't allowed in the classroom where I could learn those things, and I'd never be able to make people understand what I wanted to say.

I felt as if I was going around and around in some kind of mixed-up maze that didn't have any way out. I drew a circle in the dirt with me in the center of lots of winding paths closed off at the ends.

Sometimes when I walked down to the school with Ed in the morning, I stood outside after everyone else had gone in and stared at the back of the door. After the teacher rang the bell and the children were inside, she always waved at me like I was supposed to go home.

No matter how quietly she pulled the door closed

behind her, I always felt as if she had slammed it in my face and shut me out of the very place where I needed to be. I scratched a skeewumpus door in the dirt, shaped all out of kilter from being banged shut. Someday I intended to be on the other side of that schoolroom door.

My mind wanted to know things. It seemed to me that people's brains must be made out of different materials. Ed's and mine were as different as feathers and flypaper. His was flighty; mine was sticky. All the things that went into my head seemed to stay put in nice, neat rows. If I concentrated, I could pick out any idea and think about it again any time I wanted to.

Ed couldn't do that at all. Mama said that everything she told him went in one ear and out the other. It made me think that his ears were like two open windows, and the thoughts blew through, one at a time, like lazy feathers riding on a breeze, not touching his mind at all. I could just imagine all the wasted things he heard in the schoolroom and didn't catch. They must be whirling around outside his head like feathers after a pillow fight, floating away so he could never get them back.

He didn't want to remember a thing he was taught in school. Whenever I tried to get him to tell me about school, or to teach me to read, he said, "Forget school. It's a pain in the neck."

I couldn't forget it. I wanted to grab all those loose ideas and file them in my mind. Maybe the reason things stayed in my head so long was because they couldn't get out the usual way—through my mouth. Perhaps they were being stored in my brain just in case a miracle happened and I could talk someday. I saved words in my head, too, so I could fit the right ones together to describe my thoughts.

I drew some feathers flying in the air over the maze. They seemed to tickle the notion that was trying to take shape in my head, and I focused my thoughts on figuring out what it was. Then I remembered the sampler Mama had been encouraging me to make to show off all the embroidery stitches I had learned to do.

"It's a tradition in our family," she explained, "for every girl to make a sampler to save in her hope chest to hang on the wall when she gets married." She pointed to her "Home Sweet Home" sign done in cross-stitch.

Mama could tell what my eyes were asking and answered, "Yes, Caroline will make one, too, all in good time. But she's not as clever with her fingers as you are. Besides, she's very busy studying her school work right now."

I knew I'd rather be busy with learning lessons than doing clever things with my fingers.

"I think you can even draw some of your own

designs," Mama said. "It's much nicer to be original than to use someone else's patterns."

She was right when she said that I could draw. I looked at the line of watermelon smiles in the dirt. They would be perfect for a scalloped border on my sampler. Like a green and rosy frame wrapped all around it. Once I had the edge done, I'd have to figure out what to put inside it.

A rectangular piece of linen and all colors of embroidery thread were waiting in the little wooden treasure chest Papa had carved for my ninth birthday in August.

Maybe things would be different in New Mexico. Maybe they'd let me go to school there. If they would just allow me to be in the classroom, I'd never disturb anyone, and I could learn a lot just by listening. I always did in my Sunday School class.

Almost as if they were reading my mind, Papa and Mama began talking about church.

"Of course we'll find a church there," Papa laughed. "It was a Latter-day Saint working in the land office down there who wrote to Clem Coldwell and told him about the available land. A Brother Talbot, I think. There's already some sort of meeting-house in Clovis, and even if there weren't, enough people will be going from here to build one—a dozen families."

"Anyone else we know?"

"The Lenstroms, for sure. And I think some people from Murray have signed up."

I liked Jenny Lenstrom. She was in my Sunday School class, and her sister, Sarah, was in Caroline's.

I was thinking more about the design I was drawing than about what Papa was saying, so I only heard snatches of the conversation for a while.

"... make the land productive ... after five years ... it's ours to keep ... some brick-laying jobs ... till the first crop comes in ... warm, mild climate ..."

But when Papa said, "It'll be good not to be shoveling snow," he got my attention in a hurry.

Chapter 2

Wordless Messages

No snow? No fox and geese games? No making angels with wings or rolling up balls to build snowmen? No sleigh rides with bells jangling on the horses' harnesses? No hot spiced cider to warm us up afterwards? I felt sort of a hollow, empty place under my ribs, like the time I'd lost my lucky penny down a crack in the floor. Did I really want to leave Utah and go to New Mexico? For a minute, I wondered.

Still and all, to take the whole family and move to a different state where there would be room to grow watermelons seemed like such an exciting thing to do that I almost couldn't breathe just thinking about it. As soon as Ed got home from school and found out about it, he'd take me with him to tell all our friends.

Mama and Papa sat down on the top step and stayed there for a while just thinking. Finally Mama spoke, and she asked exactly what I wanted to know.

"How much is a hundred and sixty acres?"

"Sixteen square blocks," Papa told her. "Salt Lake City blocks, that is."

"Are Salt Lake City blocks any different from other blocks?" she asked him.

"Don't know," he said. "I just know that when Brigham Young laid out the city back in pioneer times, all the blocks were ten acres. All the streets were wide and straight with the directions of the compass."

Papa laughed. "President Young must have liked the number ten," he said. "He specified that city blocks were to be *ten* acres each and that towns were to have *ten* thousand people. And to make it convenient for travelers to find a stopping place where they could get a good meal and be safe from Indians at night, he planned for the towns to be *ten* miles apart."

"More to the point," Mama said, "is how many miles apart are Holladay, Utah, and Clovis, New Mexico?"

"Best I can figure from the map," Papa told her, "is about nine hundred miles."

"*Nine hundred miles*!" Mama gulped. "That's like the pioneers crossing the plains to Utah."

"Not quite," Papa assured her. "Only three-fourths as far. We'll travel on roads instead of trails. And we'll pass through towns along the way."

"Every ten miles?" Mama asked.

Papa laughed again. "Not in that direction, I'm afraid," he said. "But much closer than in pioneer times."

"What about Indians?" Mama sounded concerned.

Papa nodded his head. "Could see some. Lots of Indian tribes in that part of the country. But don't forget," he brightened, "that we Latter-day Saints have a good reputation with the Indians. We 'feed 'em, don't fight 'em,' remember?"

"I'd just as soon not meet any at all," Mama said.

Not Ed, I thought. He'd love to see some Indians. I scratched a man in the dirt with a bow and arrow and put feathers all around his head.

"This Clovis place must be clear on the other side of New Mexico to be nine hundred miles away," Mama said.

"Right near the Texas border," Papa agreed. "Halfway down the state."

"So what route do we take to get there?"

"What they call the Old Spanish Trail. It goes down through Price, Green River, and Moab to Monticello, then across the southwest corner of Colorado through Durango and into New Mexico as far as Santa Fe. After that, I'm not exactly sure, but probably along the Pecos River to Fort Sumner. That's where the land office is. Clovis is east of there about sixty miles."

"How long will it take?"

"If we travel twenty-five miles a day," Papa began, "it'll take . . . " He paused to do the figuring in his head. " . . . thirty-six days to go nine hundred miles. At twenty miles, it would be forty-five days. We can probably get there in five or six weeks."

"That's a long trip," Mama observed.

"Yup," Papa answered, "but this is the best time of year to go. We'll celebrate Thanksgiving on our own place this year."

While I scribbled designs in the dirt, the idea for my sampler was growing like yeast foaming in a hot kitchen. One thought bubbled up right after the other. Green buttonhole stitch would be perfect for the rind on the watermelon because then the extra material could be trimmed away to leave a scalloped edge that wouldn't fray. I could sew bright pink solid-stitch centers and speckle them with tiny black lazy-daisy seeds. I closed my eyes and imagined the brilliant border I would make.

Just then Ed's shrill whistle split the air, signaling to me that he was on his way home from school. I ran off to meet him. He could tell by my skipping steps and wide smile that I was happy about something.

"Good news?" he asked.

I grinned and bobbed my head up and down.

"Mama's making cookies?" he guessed.

I shook my head no.

"Papa gave you a penny to spend?"

I shook my head again.

"What, then?" he wanted to know.

I grabbed his hand and pulled him to the place by the back step and showed him what I'd been drawing in the dirt. He scratched his head and tried to figure it out.

"Well," he said, "it looks like lots of pieces of watermelon . . ."

I nodded my head rapidly.

" . . . and an Indian with a bow and arrow . . . and a girl in the middle of a maze."

He studied the ground some more and pointed to the skeewumpus door. "And a . . . ?"

I ran up the steps and patted the door.

"A door?"

I nodded.

"Why so crooked?"

I opened the door and slammed it shut with a loud bang.

He looked puzzled. "A slammed door?" he asked.

I agreed with a fast bob of my head.

"So what does it mean?" he wanted to know.

I wanted to explain about moving to New Mexico where maybe the schoolroom door wouldn't be slammed so I'd be able to learn to read and write and get out of the maze I was in and we'd have lots of watermelon and maybe see Indians on the way.

I pointed at him and then me and tried to say, "Move to New Mexico," and it came out more like "Mmoo Nnmmmo."

"What?" he puzzled.

"Mmoo, mmoo," I said louder.

"Cow?" he asked.

I shook my head and drew a team of horses.

"Horses," he said, "not cows."

I added a loaded-up wagon so he'd understand "move."

"Oh, I get it!" he shouted. "We're going to haul the junk to the dump! Yippee!" He was gone like a shot, calling to Papa.

I plunged through the willow wall of my playhouse and banged my fists against the tree trunk.

"It's no use!" I screamed silently to myself. "I can't make him understand. I can't tell anyone anything. Why can't I talk? Why can't I write? Why can't I go to school like everyone else? Why? It's not fair; it's just not fair!"

I beat the rough bark until the blood dripped from my skinned hands, but I didn't feel the pain. I was hurting too much deep inside me.

I cried for a long time. Until all the tears I had inside were squeezed out and dried up like a leftover lemon peel. Until I was too tired to sob even one more time. The crying didn't change anything. I still couldn't talk. But somehow it seemed as if part of the sadness had been washed away, because my heart didn't feel quite as heavy anymore.

At church on Sunday all the people were talking about the families who were going to move, and everyone was offering to help them. Brother Golden, who had a long red beard, patted me on the head, as usual. I always thought his name was the wrong color. It should have been Brother Red to match his fiery whiskers. Since he didn't hear very well, he was in the habit of asking questions and then answering them himself.

I remembered the first time I'd ever seen him, when I was just a little girl. He picked me up, and I reached out to feel his bright beard, which looked soft and silky. Instead, it was stiff and prickly, and I jerked my hand away.

"Do you like it?" he asked.

I wanted to say, "Can't you cut it off?" but my mumble was useless. He didn't notice, though. He couldn't tell that I couldn't talk.

"I thought you did," he said with a smile. "You're an angel." I wondered why he called me an angel. Maybe because I had yellow curls, blue eyes, and dimples in my cheeks. Most pictures of angels did. But most pictures of angels had wings, too, and I knew for sure that they didn't, really. We learned in

Sunday School that they can travel anywhere they want to go without them. This time Brother Golden asked, "How's my angel?" as if I were still a little girl, and then he answered himself, "Pretty as a picture."

"Do you need a cover for your wagon?" he asked Papa. "I can help you make one if you'll pick up some canvas from . . . "

Mama hurried me off to my class, and when I got there my teacher was giving leather Bibles to the children who had a hundred percent attendance for a year—black ones for the boys, white for the girls. I wanted one of those Bibles so bad I could hardly stand it. I had had only three more weeks to go to earn one when I caught the chicken pox from Caroline and missed two Sundays in a row and had to start all over. Now there was no way I could get one. I'd be gone in less than a month.

After the class, I went up to the front of the room to look at the one beautiful book that was left over—a white one. Just as I reached up to touch it, Sister Johnson turned around from taking down the pictures she'd pinned on the wall for the lesson, and I quickly pulled my hand away. She looked at me with love in her eyes.

"You're moving away soon, aren't you, Dora?"

I nodded my head.

"I'll miss having you in my class," she said. "I can tell that you feel very close to God."

She was right. I did feel close to God. I knew he could understand me even when no one else did.

"Would you like to have that Bible to take with you?" Sister Johnson asked kindly.

I bobbed my head up and down so fast I could feel my curls bouncing, and she handed me the book. I hugged it tight against my heart and looked up at her through watery eyes.

"Bless you, child," she said, then stooped to take me in her arms. She squeezed me tight for a long time before she kissed the top of my head and gave my behind a little pat to send me on my way.

I skipped from the room so happy I wished I could sing.

I was glad that Sister Johnson didn't know I couldn't read, or she might have thought that I didn't need the book. But I did need it. Having it was like a dream, a promise, that someday I would be able to read it. Already I knew many of the verses by heart. " . . . in the beginning was the Word and the Word was with God and the Word was God . . . The Lord is my shepherd; I shall not want . . . And they came with haste and found Mary and Joseph and the babe lying in the manger." It was easy for me to memorize the things I heard. But when I couldn't say them, no one could tell that I knew them. Except God. He knew. He understood.

Maybe, if I prayed enough, things would be different in New Mexico. Maybe the teacher would let me go to school there. I promised myself that whether she did or not, somehow I would learn to read that Bible and teach myself to write what I wanted to say. No matter how hard it was, I would do it.

Chapter 3

Everything Bad Has Some Good

I didn't have any trouble getting Mama to understand about the sampler. As soon as she saw me making my watermelon design around a piece of paper the same size as the cloth, she knew what I was doing.

"Good for you, Dora," she encouraged. "That's a wonderful idea for the border. Just right for a melon lover. When you finish drawing, I'll help you trace your pattern onto the cloth. But first, let me show you a little secret my mother taught me." Mama folded the paper several times, clipped the edges, and opened out the page. Nice even scallops went all around the edge. There were just enough for nine watermelon smiles across the top and bottom and thirteen along each side. All I needed to do was fill in the curved lines that marked the inside edges of the rinds, draw straight ones across to show where the pink ended, and mark black dots for the seeds.

I was busy for a long while with the pencil. Forty-four is a lot of pieces of watermelon to draw. I decided it would seem like even more by the time I'd embroidered them.

"Your sampler's going to be a real treasure," Mama said as she finished transferring my pattern onto the linen fabric. "When it's all finished, signed, and dated, Papa will make a frame for it."

I hadn't decided for sure what other pictures I would use for the center part. I folded up the pattern and put it in my box with the notepad that had my other drawings in it.

The whole family was busy getting ready to move and I had to decide which things I wanted to take in my chest.

"That's all the room you can have," Papa told me.

How could I fit all the treasures I'd collected in my nine years of life into a space smaller than a bread box? I packed and repacked it, over and over, trying to figure out the best way to get the most in, but I never could get the chest to hold all I wanted it to.

Mama and Papa were having the same problem with the wagon. "It just isn't big enough," Mama complained, "to take all we need and eight people besides."

"It will have to be," Papa told her. "We'll sell everything we don't have room for, and that'll give us some money to buy what we need when we get there. We can only take what we have to have for eating and sleeping. The wagon itself will be our shelter."

"The bed springs and mattress," Mama suggested, "can fit across the wagon box, and they will make a soft place to ride with all the quilts piled on top. We can pack lots of things underneath it."

Mama insisted that her stove had to go, too. She wasn't taking any chances about replacing it. "It takes too long to get used to a new one," she told Papa.

I knew the real reason she didn't want to go without it. I heard what she whispered when she took the bread pudding from the oven baked to the perfect shade of golden brown.

"Ah, dear and faithful friend," she told the stove, "you can cook anything just the way it ought to be done. I'm certainly not leaving you behind!"

"Dora," Papa called, "I need you to help me." He was nailing boards to the wagon so the stove wouldn't fall over and tacking straps on the sides to hold the water barrels. I sniffed the mixed smell of crisp canvas, new leather, and fresh-cut sawdust. The stove, fastened safely near the front part of the wagon with barrels full of beans and oats wedged next to it, made a solid wall behind the driver's seat.

We had to take food that wouldn't spoil: cured hams and bacon, dried beans, cheese coated with wax; potatoes, parsnips, and onions; cornmeal, oatmeal, and cracked wheat for mush; flour, sugar, salt, and spices; and some bottled fruit wrapped in dish-towels so the jars wouldn't break.

"We'll be able to hunt wild game for fresh meat," Papa said, "and take a cow along for milk and butter."

Mama packed up a few cooking utensils and some pie tins to use for plates. Papa promised her she could buy a new set of dishes in Clovis.

We filled kegs and crates, burlap bags, bushel baskets and flour sacks. It was up to Papa to fit them all in the wagon box without wasting an inch of space.

He and Mama were busy loading everything up while my best friend, Ilene, was watching me fill my chest for the last time. It didn't bother Ilene that I couldn't speak. No matter what game we played, she could keep up both ends of the conversation without hardly stopping to breathe. When she wanted to put on a play, she had a different voice for every part, and all I had to do was help her act out the story. I was getting pretty good at acting. It helped me explain what I was trying to say.

I couldn't pretend I was happy when I wasn't, though. I could feel the sad sag in my face because I had to leave my best friend behind.

I was thinking that moving from one place to another was like closing the door on a room I'd never be able to go back into again. I hated closed doors. No matter how excited I was to enter the next room in a different house down in New Mexico, part of me didn't want to go.

It made me sad to say good-bye to Ilene and the many things we shared together. I remembered the time Jake Woodrow had called me Dumb Dora.

"Dumb Dora, dumb Dora, dumb, dumb, dumb," he chanted.

Ilene whipped out at him like a coiled-up rattlesnake. "Dora's not dumb!" she hissed.

"Is too," he sassed. "Can't talk, can she?"

"Just because she can't talk doesn't mean she's dumb!" Ilene yelled at him. "She has more brains in her little finger than you have in your whole head!" She dotted the exclamation point with a fist in his stomach.

With a gasp he bent over double like a hairpin. When he got his breath again, he shot daggers of hate at her with his eyes, but he never called me Dumb Dora again.

I would miss Ilene.

"Can you get everything in the box?" she asked me. I shook my head and watched Mama hand a loaded bushel basket to Papa to put in the wagon.

"Where do you think is the best place for the chickens?" she asked.

"Chickens?" Papa groaned. "We're not taking any chickens." "Of course we are," Mama insisted. "Three or four of the best layers and Caroline's pet rooster so we can raise some chicks in the spring. And a couple of stewing hens to eat on the way."

Papa sighed. When Mama had that determined sound in her voice he knew it was no use to argue. Besides, chicken dinner was his favorite.

"I guess we can put them in a crate and tie it to the side by the washtubs. You'd better get some chicken feed."

"It's already packed," she assured him. "Will we have plenty of water?"

"We're taking two barrels," Papa told her. "One for drinking, one for washing. We'll fill them when we need to. No use hauling the extra weight if we're traveling alongside a stream."

My sampler was already folded in a neat little packet with colored thread, thimble, extra needles, and a tiny pair of scissors so I could work on it whenever I had a chance as we traveled. I set it aside to go in the top of my chest and placed the white leather Bible in the bottom. Pressed between its pages were some beautiful red leaves I'd gathered from the bright maples growing at the foot of Mount Olympus behind Grandpa's farm. I tied yarn both ways around the book so they wouldn't fall out.

Next, I dropped the seeds in a little crack that was left by the side of the book. There were eight brown beans, half a dozen watermelon seeds, and a handful of maple wings—some to plant and some to play with. Each was shaped like a long figure eight bent in the middle with one fat seed in each end, and I loved the way they fell whirling to the ground when I tossed them in the air.

Then I tucked in the long strand of tiny glass beads I had strung at Sister Johnson's. She had given them to me in a slim bottle with a cork stopper one day when Mama was visiting her. While they talked, I had picked up the beads one at a time with a thin needle and slipped them along the thread, choosing the colors to suit me as I went.

I began to fold a doll shawl small enough to fit in the other end of the box. Then I changed my mind and handed it to Ilene. I had made it myself from Mama's yarn scraps when I first learned to crochet, and it was soft and warm and cuddly. I decided that I wanted Ilene to have it to remember me by when she played with her doll. I indicated it was to be hers.

"For keeps?" she asked, and I nodded my head yes. She hugged it and tickled her cheek with the fringe, and her eyes looked the same way mine felt—sort of wet and shiny.

"Will the doll fit?" she wanted to know. I answered by placing Henrietta on the soft place I'd made with her flannel nightie. Henrietta was a beautiful painted-eye doll with china head and hands and a stuffed-leather body. Some girls had shut-eye dolls, but I wouldn't have traded because I loved Henrietta so much. I wrapped my little mirror in an old blue sweater so it wouldn't break and tucked it in the box with a couple of doll dresses. Next went my paper pad and a pencil for drawing more designs and, last of all, the sampler. That was all the chest would hold.

"What about these?" Ilene asked, pointing to the rest of my treasures beside her on the step.

I shook my head and handed them to her one by one—an old hat and a pair of shoes we used to play dress-up, some more doll clothes, and an almost-worn-out fairy-tale book. When I came to the bag of marbles, I dumped them out, selected five or six of my favorites, and pushed them into the corners of my box. I returned the rest to the bag and gave it to Ilene.

After she went home with her hands full, I noticed, again, the pain that was crawling down the side of my neck. It had started two or three days before as a tender spot behind my right ear and now was a sore and throbbing lump.

By morning I was burning up with fever and couldn't stand the pain. Mama took one look at the spot I pointed to and said, "Oh, my, that's bad. Albert, come look at this."

Papa did. "It's a great big boil, all right," he said, "nearly popping with pus. If it was anywhere else I'd treat it myself, but infections anywhere on the head are dangerous. Could drain into the brain. We'd better take her to the doctor."

The doctor? The very word scared me. No one in our family had ever been to a doctor as long as I could remember. It cost too much money. Papa took care of all the sick children and animals himself.

"What will he do?" Ed wanted to know.

"Cut it open and drain out the pus," Papa told him.

"Will it hurt?" Caroline asked.

"Probably will for a minute or two," Papa said, "but after that it will get better."

I didn't like the idea of having any part of me cut open, even if it would get better afterwards, so I ran out in the orchard to hide. After a while Papa found me and convinced me I had to go. He'd hitched the team to the nearly loaded-up wagon, and Mama was already waiting on the seat.

"I'll let you off while I go pick up the water barrels," Papa said after he pulled to a stop in front of a house with a sign hanging next to the door.

After a short talk with Mama, the doctor took a look behind my ear. "You're right," he told her. "It's an ugly boil. In a bad place. I'll have to lance it." He picked up a small knife with a sharp point, and when I pulled away, he instructed Mama to hold my head still.

"This will just feel like a little pin prick," he explained. "It will be over before you can say 'Jack Robinson.' "

Right when he said the name, I felt the prick and then a warm stream running down my neck. He mopped up the yellow pus with a piece of cotton.

"There, now," he said, "that wasn't so bad, was it?"

I wanted to say, "Bad enough," but couldn't, of course, so I said nothing.

"Cat got your tongue?" he teased me.

I shook my head.

"She can't talk much," Mama told him.

"Can't talk? Why not?" the doctor wanted to know and looked into my mouth to see if he could tell what was wrong. "Why, she's tongue-tied," he said.

"What's that?" Mama wanted to know.

"I'll show you," the doctor said, and Mama looked in my mouth too.

"See how her tongue is fastened down to the bottom of her mouth?" He poked at it with a flat stick. "She can't lift it at all. No wonder she can't talk. It just bumps up in the middle of her tiny mouth and makes mush out of everything she tries to say."

He's right about that, I thought.

"It's a very simple procedure to correct it," the doctor told us. "It should have been done a long time ago." He explained that all he had to do was to cut my tongue loose, and then I'd be able to talk like everyone else.

I couldn't believe it! It looked as if the prayer I'd prayed all my life was finally going to be answered, and all because I'd had such an awful pain. I guess what Mama said over and over again must be true: "Everything bad always has something good about it."

A rosy future flashed before my eyes in an instant like some kind of vision. I was living in a new house surrounded by a pink and green watermelon patch and talking like everyone else. The slammed schoolroom door was left behind in Utah, and an open one, inviting me inside, beckoned ahead in New Mexico. I saw the whole happy picture like a framed sampler hanging on the wall.

The doctor asked Mama when would be a good time for the operation, and she said, "You'd better do it now. We're leaving tomorrow."

I had forgotten the rest of Mama's favorite saying: "And everything good has some bad." The bad was awful. Cutting my tongue loose was just the beginning.

Chapter 4

Everything Good Has Some Bad

Fixing my tongue may have seemed like a simple thing to the doctor, but it was a great big pain to me. Simply awful, in fact.

He showed Mama how she needed to hold my head still while he did the cutting and told me he'd drop some ether on my tongue to make it numb so I couldn't feel anything.

"Open wide," he instructed while he unscrewed the lid of a small jar and sucked up some liquid in an eyedropper. He drizzled it on my tongue. It felt freezing cold at first and smelled sickly sweet.

Before long my mouth felt like it had gone to sleep, and my head was woozy. The room seemed to spin in a foggy blur, and I started to feel dead all over. He was right. I couldn't feel anything while he operated.

Sometimes I woke up a little and heard some

faraway voices talking. The only words I remember are "very severe case."

My tongue was still pretty numb when he finished wiping up the blood and said, "Such a brave young lady surely deserves to have a piece of candy to suck on to get rid of that awful ether taste."

He pulled a nickel from his pocket and handed it to me. A nickel. A whole nickel! I'd never ever had more than a penny to spend for candy before, and I knew exactly what I wanted to buy—the biggest piece of peppermint in the store. I wouldn't have to share it with anyone or nibble it slowly to make it last. I'd have enough to just go right ahead and chew it up to enjoy the delicious crunchiness. I pulled Mama quickly across the street to the store, anxious to pop the candy into my mouth.

As soon as I took the first big bite, I could tell I'd made the wrong choice. There was something wrong with the candy. It didn't crack between my teeth the way it should. It felt kind of tough and leathery and had sort of a salty taste, like when I sucked my finger after a cut. I'd forgotten how peppermint can sting, and it burned like fire under my tongue.

I wanted to spit it out and I felt the juice dribbling down my chin, so I tugged at Mama's sleeve to ask for a handkerchief. When she turned to see what I wanted, she gasped.

"What happened, Dora? You're bleeding again!" The numbness was wearing off more and more, and my tongue was hurting. The pain got worse and worse.

Mama rushed me back to the doctor, and after he looked in my mouth, he said, "Oh, dear, she's chewed her tongue. It looks like a piece of raw meat. Didn't I warn you about that?"

"No," Mama said in a voice made of ice, "you didn't."

"Well, she's learned the hard way," the doctor said. Then he explained to me what had happened.

"Most people's tongues know how to keep away from their teeth from the beginning, but yours was tied down where it wasn't in any danger. Now that it's cut loose, it can easily get between those sharp choppers and, unless you are very careful, you will bite it.

"Do you have any ice?" he asked Mama.

What he meant was did we have any ice left in our ice house from last winter, or had it all melted.

"More than we need," Mama assured him. "Albert always packs it in plenty of sawdust."

"Then give her some ice chips to suck on to keep the swelling down," the doctor said. "And remember," he said, pointing his finger at me, "that I said *suck*, not chew. I believe that's what I said about the candy, too."

When he mentioned it, I remembered that he had.

He gave me some pills to take for the pain, warned me again to be careful when I ate, and told me to rinse my mouth out with warm salt water.

If there was anything I hated, it was salt water. It always reminded me of the day the family went to Black Rock to go swimming in Great Salt Lake. It was the end of June, and we were going to celebrate Mama's birthday. But the dewberries needed to be picked before we could go, so Caroline, Ed, and I went to work to get the job done in a hurry.

Mama warned us girls to cover our arms with one of Papa's old shirts and to wear stockings on our legs to protect them from the thorns, but I was too anxious to finish to bother with that. Besides, it was too hot with all those extra clothes on. I even forgot about using a stick to lift up the long, prickly vines, and they seemed to reach out to snag me on purpose. Soon I was covered with little stinging scratches.

When we got to the beach and I walked into the lake, my skin felt like a fire had been started under it. I splashed my way out as fast as I could, and the salty water flew into my eyes, burning them as well.

There was no fresh water to wash off in, only the scalding, dry salt caking onto my body as the water dried up and the hot sand scorching my feet until I had to dance as fast as I could from one to the other so my soles didn't get fried.

The worst part was pretending nothing was wrong. I already knew it was my own fault for not wearing the stockings and shirt in the berry patch. I didn't want to be reminded of my disobedience by anyone else. Besides, I didn't want to spoil Mama's birthday.

Finally I remembered that I *had* worn my shoes, so I didn't have any scratches on my feet. I stepped cautiously into the shallow water next to the edge of the lake to let them cool off.

Mama was floating around like a ripe cucumber in the irrigation ditch, laughing because her feet couldn't sink. "Isn't this fun?" she said. "I just love the way the salty water holds you up."

I walked away along the beach so I couldn't hear her coaxing me to come in. At last I found a shady spot behind the big Black Rock where I could brush the salt away from my sizzling skin while I waited to go home.

It seemed like longer than forever before everyone was tired of swimming. Then we had a picnic on the beach. The salty, sandy grit got mixed into the food and even ruined the watermelon.

I didn't want anything to do with salt water ever again after that, and I had no intention of using it to rinse my sore tongue. But Mama insisted. Just as I expected, it stung worse than the peppermint, and I closed my mouth tight and refused to open it.

"What you need," Mama said later in the day, "is some nice warm broth. I'll just kill one of those chickens we don't have room to take and make some for you."

"It'll do you good," she coaxed as she placed a steaming bowl in front of me at supper time. "It will flow right under your sore tongue, and the heat will help to heal it."

I wouldn't even try the golden liquid.

"No salt," Mama promised, "and nothing to chew."

Cautiously I dipped out a spoonful and blew it cool enough so it didn't burn. The first sip tasted pretty good so I had some more, and it did make my hollow stomach feel better. I finished most of what Mama had given me, and she put the rest in quart jars to take with us.

"We'll need to pack it in ice so it won't spoil," she told Papa.

After supper Mama sent us over to Grandma's to get a good night's sleep before we left. Everything at our place was packed except for the table and chairs.

"We can't take them," Papa said. "There's just no more room."

"Oh, Albert," Mama cried, "we can't get along without a place to eat."

"I know, Hon," he agreed. "I promise I'll make some new ones as soon as we get there."

I noticed that Mama held her lips together tight, like she was afraid she might say something she'd be sorry for, and then she straightened her shoulders as if she were getting ready to carry a heavy load.

For the first time I wondered if she really wanted to move.

Chapter 5

But with Joy Wend Your Way

Our wagon train left for New Mexico on Monday morning, October third. All twelve of the families who were going met together in Murray, just south of Salt Lake City. The relatives and close friends we were leaving behind gathered there, too, to see us off.

Brother Coldwell, who was in charge and would lead the company, assigned each wagon a place in line, handed out maps, and explained the rules of the trail. We were in the third position, following the Lenstroms. Two men on horseback rode as scouts to check the road ahead, locate our camping spots, and hunt for game when we needed meat.

After the men took care of dividing up the daily duties, we all stood in a big circle for one last prayer together. Most everyone had some tears shining in their eyes when we finally started off and waved a final good-bye.

With all that crying and good-byeing, I was glad that I already knew how to keep my mouth shut when I was excited. That was the only way I could be sure not to chew on my tongue again. It was still plenty sore from the day before.

Two big boys were making a loud ruckus, and I hoped they weren't going with us, but at the last minute they jumped up on each side of one of the drivers behind us.

"Brownlys," Papa said.

Soon we heard Brother Lenstrom's fiddle screech a long sigh, and his deep voice began booming:

> Come, come, ye Saints,
> No toil nor labor fear;
> But with joy wend your way . . .

Everyone knew this old pioneer song and the message of hope expressed in the final lines, "All is well, all is well."

The sound of the song passed from one wagon to the next as each traveler heard the encouraging words and stately tempo of the music and joined in the singing. I noticed that Brother Lenstrom skipped right over the verse that said, "And should we die before our journey's through," and, in an extra loud voice, started at the beginning again.

By then all sadness at leaving was gone, and we were all happy to be on our joyful way toward the place that held the promise of a good new life for us—just like the old-time pioneers who crossed the plains coming west to Utah.

The first two nights we could see the advantages of Brigham Young's plan to have towns close enough for travelers to find convenient stopping places. Our scouts rode ahead to make arrangements for each of the traveling families to stay at a different home. Church members, first in Lehi and then in Springville, knew we were coming and welcomed us warmly with home-cooked meals and overnight lodgings.

The roast beef and pan-browned potatoes at the Jensens' in Springville looked and smelled so good that I wanted to gobble them up like everyone else did, but my mouth was still too sore to try chewing yet. Mama heated up some of the chicken broth for me, and Sister Jensen gave me an extra big helping of the smooth, nutmeg-flavored custard she'd baked for dessert. It slid easily over my sore tongue and tasted delicious.

"How long will it take us to get to Price from here?" Papa inquired at breakfast the next morning.

"About six or seven days," Brother Jensen said. "The road over Soldier Summit is pretty steep in some places—especially going down into Helper."

"Are we ready for a week of camping out?" Papa asked Mama when we walked out to the wagon to leave. "This is our last chance for a long while to get any supplies."

"I wish we had a bushel of apples," Mama said, and just then, like a genie in a bottle making her wish come true, Brother Jensen came up out of the cellar carrying a basket of tart, crispy Jonathans that made my mouth water. Just the thought of chewing them, though, reminded me of the pain caused by the peppermint stick. I held my mouth shut tight.

"Do you think you'd have room to take a second bushel, for my brother's family in Price?" Brother Jensen asked.

"Of course we would," Papa told him, leaning into the wagon to see where we could put them.

Every crack had been packed, so both of the baskets had to sit on top of the bed with all of us children. It made us so crowded we hardly had room to move, but at least we could reach for a crunchy snack whenever we wanted one.

The good smell of the tempting fruit made me starving hungry to have some, but I didn't dare take a bite. Finally, I broke an apple in half and sucked up the delicious juice. It tasted so good that I scraped off tiny bits with my top teeth and swallowed them without chewing.

The sunny autumn days were beautiful—so brisk

and cool in the morning that everyone was anxious to start moving, warm enough in the afternoon to make the little children drowse off.

That's when I leaned against an apple basket and stitched on my sampler. The watermelon-wedge border became brighter and brighter as I finished one section, then another. I decided to finish one scallop every day. That way I could keep track of how long it took to get to New Mexico.

While I sewed, I tried out shifting my tongue around. It felt strange to be able to move it into any part of my mouth. I could even stick it out in front, the way Ed did when he was being sassy. I could stretch it up almost to my nose and down toward my chin. I dug the mirror out of my chest to see, for the first time, what my tongue looked like. I'd never been able to inspect it before. It was sort of rough on the top with a crack down the middle, and streaky-stripey on the bottom when I lifted it up.

We took turns riding with Papa on the driver's seat. From there we could look at everything that was up ahead. When we rode in the back of the wagon, we couldn't see anything until we'd already passed it, or, if the canvas sides were rolled up, we could look sideways.

The third day out of Springville, it was my turn to be in front with Papa and George. Already the country looked different from the Salt Lake Valley.

What had happened to the high, rocky mountains like the ones that stood guard over our yard in Holladay? And where was the heavy growth of aspens and pines we had in our canyons? What made the dirt the color of rusty nails? I had so many questions that I needed to ask. I pointed around, hoping Papa could figure out what I wanted to know.

"Sure is good deer country," he told me as he followed my finger with his eyes. "Wouldn't be surprised if we have venison for supper one of these days."

The cottonwoods growing along the stream glistened like gold in the Indian-summer sunlight. We were close to a railroad track and often passed long trains loaded with black lumps of coal.

"From Price," Papa told me, "where the coal mines are."

We counted the cars together, Papa and George naming the numbers, me just saying them in my mind. And we waved at the man who looked at us out the window behind the engine.

When we stopped at night, the wagons were pulled into a safe, tight circle surrounding the campfires. Then it was that most of the children got some time to play.

Lucky for me I had grabbed my jump rope from a nail behind the back door at the last minute before we left home. It was like a strand of golden magic, it made so much difference in the way the other children treated me.

Suddenly I was the most popular girl in the camp because everyone wanted to share it. No one expected me to talk with a sore mouth, and they found out that I didn't need to. Our wagon soon became the favorite gathering place for most of the children in the camp.

As soon as the wagons were parked, the girls came shouting, "My turn with the jump rope, Dora!"

"No, it's mine," someone else would challenge while we yanked up the sagebrush to clear a playing place.

"I'll let you have a cookie," Martha bargained. She always carried cookies to barter for a turn and, since she couldn't jump very long anyway, usually found someone willing to trade.

When it was decided who could go first, the rest began to chant:

> Mo-ther Hub-bard sat on a pin.
> How many inch-es did it go in?
> One, two, three, four . . .

As long as the jumper didn't miss a beat, it was her turn, but when she did, she gave up the rope to another. If she jumped past twenty, the others began to call out:

> Ma-ble, Ma-ble, set the ta-ble,

And don't for-get the RED HOT PEPPER!

At this signal the rope started whirring at double time. No one could last forever on red hot pepper.

While I clapped to the chant of the others, I wanted to capture the happy moments and keep them forever. I imagined how I could embroider girls in cross-stitch dresses jumping over yarn ropes anchored with couching stitch, or another group scratching a hopscotch in the dirt, numbering the squares, and tossing their markers.

Maybe I'd even put Ed on my sampler, playing marbles made with round french knots. Each boy carried his favorite taw for shooting in the right-hand pocket of his overalls and, in the other, a handful of aggies that he didn't mind risking on a game of keeps.

As soon as Ed's pockets were bulging with the marbles he'd won, he would shout, "Let's play *break the record*!" and his playmates would race off to the tailgate of our wagon to begin jumping.

One for the money,
Two for the show,
Three to get ready,
And four to go!

A line was marked where the jumper's feet landed, and each boy tried to go past the farthest mark. They had to jump sideways off the corner that faced out of the campground circle or they might hit the next wagon parked close behind ours. The big Brownly boys from Murray could jump the farthest and shout the loudest.

The men gathered brush and some bits of coal from along the railroad tracks to make the campfires hot. Then they milked the cows and fed the stock while the ladies unpacked their heavy skillets and Dutch ovens and cooked grated potatoes, sliced ham, and fried scones.

After dinner the children were put to bed and sometimes the grown-ups would dance. From the place where we slept under the wagon we could watch them whirl in a fast polka or line up for the Virginia reel while Brother Lenstrom played his fiddle.

"We're just like the old-time pioneers," Ed reminded me.

I wondered if any old-time pioneer girls had started out the journey with a cut tied tongue that was sore like mine.

Chapter 6

Baby Talk

We had traveled for nearly a week without coming to a town and, as Papa had predicted, we enjoyed some good meals of venison.

Gradually the soreness in my mouth began to heal. Bit by bit and bite by bite, I worked at teaching my tongue to stay where it belonged to avoid the sharp edges of my teeth. I hadn't made any effort to talk yet. I pretended my mouth was still sore so no one would expect me to.

It seemed strange that, as much as I wanted to speak, I was deathly afraid to try it. What if I still couldn't do it even with my tongue cut? What if everyone laughed at me and teased me? I wished I could be alone somewhere to try out my words in private and hear what they sounded like. But even alone, would I dare? I wanted to be back home in Holladay in my willow-tree playhouse. There's certainly no place to be by yourself in a covered wagon.

One morning when we loaded up to be on our way, a long train went chugging by. As it passed, Ed noticed something. "Hey," he said, "the engine's on the back end. In fact, there's two engines trailing along behind."

"Not trailing," Papa corrected him. "Pushing. Pushing hard to help that heavy load get up the steep slope. They're called 'helper engines,' and the town where they are hooked on is named Helper for that very reason."

He began hitching up the horses for our ride down the same hill the train was going up.

"Next time one comes by," Papa told us, "listen to the sound the engines make as they labor along. The one in front will say, 'heav-y pull-ing, Help-er Can-yon, heav-y pull-ing, Help-er Can-yon,' and the ones behind will whisper, 'heav-y push-ing, Help-er Can-yon, heav-y push-ing, Help-er Canyon.'

"Those are good words to remember when you have a hard task to do. And don't forget that if you help each other like the engines do, difficult jobs will be easier."

I chanted the train refrain over and over in my head, waiting to listen for it when the next load of coal came along. Soon I was humming a tune to match the words, and Mama said, "You sound happy, today."

"Umhmm," I hummed.

"Your mouth must feel better."

I nodded.

"Can you talk, then?" Ed wanted to know.

I shook my head hard and looked at Mama. I could tell she understood that I didn't want to be asked that question yet.

"Why not?" Caroline demanded.

"She's not ready to," Mama told them. "And," she added emphatically, "I don't want anyone bothering her about it until she is. Do you understand?"

Caroline and Ed both nodded, and I decided that the first sentence I wanted to say was, "I love Mama."

The road ahead was so steep that sometimes we had to get out of the wagons and walk to make it easier for the horses to go down. I wondered if we shouldn't be doing just the opposite of the train engines – pushing back on the front end and pulling in the back to slow them down a little.

"Going down such a steep hill," Papa said, sweat dripping off his face as he pulled hard on the brake, "can be harder work than going up."

Finally we came into the funny town of Helper, which had just one street winding down through the middle and steep, castle-shaped mountains on both sides.

I thought we'd stop there for sure, but when Mama asked Papa about it he said, "Nope. There're too many saloons and foreigners here. Price is just ahead, and we need to deliver those apples."

It was late by the time we got to the Jensens' place, but the house still smelled like bread fresh from the oven, and the dinner of bottled-meat gravy on biscuits was delicious. Hungry as I was, I didn't bite my tongue even once.

The Jensens were anxious to hear all about their relatives in Springville and seemed to be starved to death for apples.

Before we left Price, Papa found a place to gather some green reeds for weaving. He collected an armful, tied them in hanks, and fastened them to the side of the wagon.

My baby brother was making me ashamed of myself. Little Howie was learning to talk. And I wasn't. It embarrassed me that a baby could do what I didn't dare try. For a long time he'd been making gargling and cooing noises. Now, all of a sudden, he was saying "Mu-mu, da-da, mooooo," and calling me "Doh-wah." Everyone was making a big fuss about how darling he was. Because he was just a baby, what he did was cute.

I knew they were just as anxious to have me talk, but I surely didn't want them to make a big fuss when I did. I just wanted to talk in sentences like everyone else my age, naturally and easily, like I'd been doing it forever.

I didn't know how to begin, though. I knew that if I started the way Howie did, I'd sound like a baby, and that would give meanies like the Brownly boys something else to tease me about. No nine-year-old girl likes to be called a baby.

The more I thought about it, though, the more I figured out that Howie's method might be the only way to learn to talk. If only he could show me how, right now, while he was doing it—in some secret place, where no one could hear the mistakes I might make. I thought about that a lot, and finally I knew what I had to do.

The baby always needed to be tended while Mama cooked the supper. Sometimes I did it, and once in a while Ed got the job, but he usually had to milk the cow. Mostly Caroline was in charge of Howie because she was the oldest and he was what Mama called "a handful," especially since he'd started running everywhere he went. After a day of riding in the wagon, we were all anxious to stretch our legs.

I decided that I should be the one to take care of the baby. While everyone else was busy working or playing, I could study how he moved his mouth to make the different sounds, and I could try them out. That night I took Howie from Caroline and handed her the jump rope.

I knew I'd have a problem getting Howie to sit still long enough for me to look at his lips unless he was tired, so I coaxed him to run quite a distance from the wagons. When I could tell he was getting worn out, I rolled him down on the ground and tickled him until he was giggling, and then I made funny faces at him.

He laughed and chattered while I watched where his tongue went and imitated what he did. Soon I was making some of the same sounds. "Ma-ma. Da-da. Doh-wah." I decided that it was all right to talk baby talk to a baby. He loved it.

It was hard work, though, to make my tongue move about so much and so fast. Before long it was tired. Now I'm not tongue-tied, I thought, I'm tongue-tired. Howie was still babbling like he'd never run out of steam.

We traveled for several days through hot, dry desert, and then, right in the middle of nowhere, we came to the bustling town of Green River. Or maybe it should be called a city. Trains came and went, carrying people, cattle, coal, and ore. Stockyards were full of steers waiting to be shipped to market. New brick stores were going up on Main Street, and the elegant, three-story Palmer House Hotel with pointed gables and fountains in front was the prettiest and biggest building we'd seen yet. A new three-span bridge made of concrete, steel, and wood was almost finished across the wide river; it was scheduled to be opened and dedicated on December tenth. We could see the ferryboats that carried wagons over when the water was high, but now it was low and the horses could easily pull us through to the other side.

Just past Green River were some humpy gray hills shaped like elephant feet. After that, we saw many deep gullies that Papa called *arroyos*. They were cut in the sandy soil, he explained, by occasional heavy rains. The mountains were mostly far away and flat on the top—except for the wonderful, crazy, fanciful, red-rock mountains just before we got to Moab.

How, I wondered, did God make them? It looked as if he'd carved a soft batch of rust-colored soap into all sorts of in-and-out, round-about statues with his pocketknife and then put them in the hot sun to dry into hard rocks. The leftover scraps were still scattered all over the ground. I drew some of the fancy figures in my notebook.

It seemed as if the reddish-brown dye hadn't been mixed in very well and some of it had settled to the bottom, leaving a darker layer below a lighter one. Shiny, chocolate-colored streaks dripped down from the top like molasses spilled from a bottle.

In other places the rocks looked as if God had cooked up a big batch of brown-sugar candy, beat it until it was creamy, and, just before it hardened, spooned it out in big round dollops all over the hills.

Sometimes I took my Bible out of the box for a

little while and held it while I remembered some verses I had memorized. "And in the beginning God created the heaven and the earth . . . and God saw that it was good . . ."

I often thought that God must have enjoyed creating the world. He must have felt the same warm, happy feeling that I got when all the stitches on a watermelon slice were perfectly even.

We had to cross the Colorado River at Moab on a long, flat boat pulled by cables. It wasn't as wide as Green River, but much deeper. Workers had already started to build a bridge across the place where the stream came through the chiseled, red-rock mountains, but it wasn't done yet. The river meandered back and forth as if it couldn't make up its mind which way to go before it finally decided to disappear around another mountain.

In Moab, we were once again welcomed into the homes of Latter-day Saints, fed good meals, and put to sleep in real beds. Everyone seemed as anxious to have visitors stop as we were to have a change from our pioneer routine. Papa gathered more reeds from the marshy place near the river and fastened them to the wagon.

Day after day, I learned new sounds from Howie. "Boo, oops, no, i-yi-yi." His mouth stretched wide like a yawn to say "aw." "G-g-g" stayed deep in his throat. His lips popped open fast to make a "p" sound.

I copied what he did and was careful to do it where no one else could hear. I didn't want to spoil the surprise I was planning.

I was determined that my first sentence would be, "I love Mama," spoken privately, to her alone. I made up my mind that after that I would say whatever I could to other family members and wait a while to talk to others.

But I had a problem. Since Howie couldn't make the "l" sound, I didn't know how, either. The best I could do was, "I wuv Mama." I intended to say it right or not at all.

I decided there were quite a few things Howie didn't know yet about talking—some things I needed to learn from someone else. Figuring out how to speak and doing it was a hard job—like getting a train up a steep canyon. I thought of the heav-y-pull-ing-heav-y-push-ing-engine song and knew that I needed another helper. Then, like a little miracle, without even asking, I had one.

Chapter 7

"I Love Mama"

Almost like she knew what I needed to know, Mama started singing "La, la, la" songs to Howie. They were the same tunes as she used to sing "Swing, Baby, Swing," and "Lullaby and Good Night," but now she sang just "la, la, la," all the way through. She looked right into Howie's eyes and moved her mouth carefully as if she were trying to teach him to sing. Or say "l," I decided.

I watched the way she opened her lips and moved her tongue up and down. I noticed that it stopped just a tiny minute behind her top teeth while she said the "l" sound. I ran away to try it.

I tried and tried, again and again, and finally I had it.

That evening while everyone else was playing and Mama was busy stirring gravy over the campfire, I tiptoed quietly in back of her and hugged her from behind. I can still remember the rough feel of the nubby wool of her sweater against my cheek and her sweet smile as she turned to see who it was. Quickly, before my intent to speak could fail me, I blurted out, "I love Mama."

She dropped the spoon, spun around and grabbed me in her arms, and hugged me so hard I couldn't breathe. "Oh, Dora," she whispered with a sob in her voice, "you *can* talk. You can! Bless you, child."

Tears were shining in her eyes when she let me go and said, "You've been planning that surprise for a long time, haven't you?"

I nodded.

"Let's go find Papa right now and tell him," she said.

I shook my head, put my finger to my lips, and said, "Shh."

"Oh," she said, "I understand. You want to surprise him yourself."

I nodded. I could say, "I love Papa," too, and ran to look for him right then. He was hobbling the horses for the night so they couldn't wander away and get lost. When I got close enough, I called, "Pa-pa, Pa-pa," and he looked up, laughed out loud, and opened his arms for me to run into.

"Say that again," he whispered as he squeezed me tight.

"Pa-pa, Pa-pa," I said. "I love Papa."

"Hallelujah! Hosanna! And hip-hip-hooray!" he shouted. "My darling Dora can talk. At last I'm going to find out what's been going on inside that busy little head of yours all these years." He ruffled my hair fondly.

"Does Mama know?" he asked.

I nodded.

"Ed and Caroline?" he asked.

"No," I said.

"Then let's go tell them," he said and tugged me toward camp without noticing that I was shaking my head.

"Oh, come on," he coaxed, when I pulled back. "They've been waiting patiently for a long time and deserve to know."

I had to admit he had a point, so I went with him.

Once Ed and Caroline found out I could say a few words, they expected me to be able to talk like anyone else. They soon found out I couldn't. Mama wouldn't let them tease me about it, though. Ed was especially anxious to help me learn.

Every night, after we stopped, Papa would mark on the map how far we had traveled. I was always amazed that such a long day made such a short mark on the page, a little line that didn't tell anything about whether the road went up or down or what it looked like along the way. Or how hot it was getting. It seemed like Fourth-of-July weather, not like it was nearly Halloween.

I was counting the days myself with the watermelon scallops on the edge of my sampler. I had done twenty-one when we came to Monticello, and was hoping we could find a store to buy more pink embroidery thread. Mine was almost all used up.

"This may be the last Latter-day Saint town we come to," Papa told Mama. "And good-bye to Utah. We have to make up our minds here which route to take."

"I thought that was decided before we started," she said.

"I did too," Papa agreed. "But there seems to be a difference of opinion. Some people favor going south through thc LDS settlements along the San Juan River so we won't leave the church hospitality behind so soon. Others think we should cut across the corner of Colorado and continue to follow the old Spanish Trail. Either way, the next stretch is going to be hot and dry."

"Do you think we can get some ice?" Mama wanted to know. She asked the same question every time we came to a town, and we usually found some. Mama liked to keep the extra cream cool until she'd saved enough to churn it into butter.

We spent a pleasant night eating, sleeping, and visiting with the Barlow family. In the morning they loaded us down with a couple of loaves of homemade bread, a bag of molasses cookies, and some fresh fried chicken for a picnic.

I had some new embroidery thread for my sampler, too. At first I was disappointed that it wasn't quite the same shade of pink as I'd been using, but when Mama reminded me that melons don't match either, I didn't mind quite so much.

No one seemed in much of a hurry to leave. The women were visiting as if they'd never have another chance to talk to anyone again, and the wagon-train leaders were busy talking about the trail ahead.

I pricked up my ears when I heard Brother Coldwell say, "That could be a problem."

I wondered what could be a problem. Then Papa said, "We might meet some between here and Cortez. This is Indian country, you know."

Indians! My skin popped out in goose bumps, and my heart banged double time in my crowded chest.

"What could we do?" Brother Lenstrom asked.

"Act friendly," Papa suggested.

"Keep smiling," Brother Coldwell added.

"Would it help if I played a cheery tune on my fiddle?" Brother Lenstrom asked.

"Probably would," Papa agreed, "and . . . "

I could tell by the way he left the words hanging in the air without dropping his voice to end the sentence that he was figuring out something in his head.

Finally he said, "I know what we can do," but I didn't find out what it was because he began to speak like he was telling a secret. The three men crouched down on their haunches while he sketched something in the dirt. After a while they all got up and went in different directions.

Even though it wasn't wash day, Papa put some water in the wash barrel. Then he unfastened all the reeds he'd gathered and dropped them in too.

"Wha fo?" I asked.

"Just in case I need them," he said.

Could they have anything to do with the plan Papa had figured out? I wondered.

It was nearly noon before everyone was ready to leave.

"The Colorado-mesa route looked like the shortest way," Papa explained as he harnessed up the horses. "Our wagon will lead today."

"How come?" Mama wanted to know.

"Just because," Papa told her.

"Just because why?" Mama persisted.

"*Just because*," Papa said firmly in his I-can't-tell-you-that-right-now voice. I knew he didn't want to get her all upset by mentioning Indians.

"What about ice?" Mama asked coolly, changing the subject.

"On the way out of town," Papa replied, "is an ice house."

He bought a big chunk, put it in a washtub, and handed Mama the ice pick so she could chip off pieces for all of us to suck on.

She had decided she wanted to ride inside the wagon out of the sun, so Ed and I climbed up in front and sat next to Papa on the driver's seat. All we could see was desert in every direction, covered with sagebrush, rabbit brush, and dried-up grass. There was not a tree in sight.

The October sun was hot. Heat waves curled up in ghostly spirals. Reflected sun shimmered and danced across the wide wasteland. Clouds of choking dust followed the wagons and the drivers behind us slowed down a little to let it settle some.

After a while Papa stopped the wagon to give the horses a drink.

"They're doing all the work in this heat," he said. "They need plenty of water."

"You do too," he told us and brought out two tin cups filled with ice chips for Ed and me. By then, Coldwells' and Lenstroms' wagons had stopped behind ours and the three men had a short conversation before Papa climbed back onto the seat and clucked to the horses to start up again.

"Look, Papa," Ed said. "There's a pond up there. We could have waited to water the horses."

"A pond?" Papa sounded surprised. "In the desert?"

"Yes. See that water up there?"

I could see it, too, and pointed to show Papa.

"See, Papa," I said.

"Oh, yes," he said with a sound in his voice that made me think he knew something we didn't. "We'll stop when we get to it."

We all kept watching and watching, but the pond didn't seem to get any closer. Finally Papa said, "Let's find out about that water. See that dark spot?" He pointed. "The one that's just even with the wet place?"

"I see it," Ed said, and I nodded that I did too.

"I see," I said.

"When we come to that we should be right where the water is, shouldn't we?"

"Yeah," Ed agreed. "Can we stop to wade in it to cool off our feet?"

"Sounds like a good idea," Papa said.

I wiped the sweat from my forehead and looked forward to a refreshing splash. As we got closer, we could tell that the dark spot was a group of trees, but when the wagon pulled up even with them the ground was as dry as ever.

"Want to go wading here?" Papa teased.

We could see the pool still further down the road. I couldn't understand what was happening. Neither could Ed.

"Hey," he said, "how come we never catch up to it?"

"Because it's not really water," Papa said. "It's only a mirage."

"What's a mirage?" Ed asked.

"A strange effect that sometimes happens in the desert," Papa explained. "Something about the layers of hot air causes a reflection of the sky and it looks like water shimmering in the sand. Lots of travelers have been fooled by it. Many have died of thirst thinking they would soon be to water."

No wonder, I thought. It had surely fooled me. The sun and sand were playing tricks on us, all right. It was hotter than ever. I was glad we had water in the barrels and some ice even if it was melting fast.

A few minutes later Ed said, "There's a people mirage."

"A what?" Papa asked.

"A people mirage. Looks like two somebodies up there shimmering in the sand." Maybe ideas flew in and out of Ed's head like feathers on the breeze, but there was certainly nothing wrong with his eyesight. I could barely see two dark spots far in the distance, but all of a sudden my curls felt as if they wanted to stand straight up. My heart started hammering so hard I could feel it in my ears. Could it be . . . ?

I continued to watch, but the shapes didn't fade or keep moving ahead of us as the mirage did. They became larger and seemed to multiply as we got closer. First it looked like two people, then four, then more. They appeared to be on horses. I grabbed Papa's arm.

"Oh-oh," Papa said.

"Oh-oh, what?" Ed asked him.

"You'll find out sooner than you want to," Papa warned.

Chapter 8

In Indian Country

"Indians!" Ed gasped, sounding scared, not excited.

Just at that moment I heard a shriek that curdled my blood. Cold shivers climbed up my backbone. Ed's "people mirage" was not at all imaginary and became a fast-moving cloud of dust racing toward us.

"Stay calm and don't worry," Papa said as he guided the wagon off the road and jumped down to the ground.

Half a dozen bronze-colored riders on spotted horses pulled to a sudden stop and scowled down at Papa, who was smiling as wide as he could.

"Friend," he greeted them and offered his hand. "Friend."

The braves continued to stare wordlessly for a moment. Then they began shouting and waving their arms.

Papa shook his head as if he didn't understand and repeated the same word again, "Friend."

He gestured toward the wagon and moved cautiously in that direction, followed by the Indians. He climbed up and reached down into the wash barrel and very slowly pulled out a hank of dripping reeds.

I decided that he didn't want to alarm the Indians by making any fast movements. They looked as puzzled as I felt. I couldn't believe what Papa did next.

He sat down on the ground and started to weave. It surely seemed like a silly time and place to make a basket.

Coldwells' wagon pulled quietly next to ours.

The braves kept watching both directions as Papa slowly laced the strips into a flat mat. One growled something I couldn't understand.

Papa said nothing but kept on with his work.

Brother Coldwell approached silently.

The Indian spoke again.

Papa nodded to acknowledge that he had heard but stayed where he was. Nothing moved but his hands as he bent the ribs up and continued to weave until a basket began to take shape.

The angry expression on the Indian speaker's face changed to curiosity. He slid off his pony and moved nearer, and the other riders followed his lead. Papa gestured to them to be seated, and they folded down in a cross-legged circle around him. Not a word was spoken.

Brother Lenstrom's wagon approached and moved next to Coldwells'. I could see our usual nighttime circle starting to form.

A soft sigh came from Brother Lenstrom's fiddle, and Papa handed the basket to one of the braves, who wove one round and then passed it to the next man in the circle.

The music began so quietly that it blended with the whisper of the breeze through the desert grasses, and the rhythm was the same as the in-and-out twining of the weavers. The basket went around and around the circle, Papa feeding in new strands as they were needed, Brother Lenstrom gradually increasing the tone and tempo of his tune. The music seemed to flow into the blood of the weavers because they began to sway back and forth and their moving arms and hands looked like dancers.

The fourth wagon pulled into place, then the fifth.

When the basket was six or seven inches from the top, Papa curved the pliable upright ribs into a looped border, tucked in the ends, and set it down in the center of the circle. Then he started another basket, and while it went from brave to brave, he began another. Then another, and another, until each Indian had his own.

When Papa stood up to get more materials, he signaled to Ed and me to climb down from the wagon. We slipped off the seat to the ground and watched quietly. Papa put the rest of the wet reeds inside the finished basket so the workers could help themselves, then stepped back and took my hand.

As the other wagons approached, one at a time, they stopped at their appointed places and the men climbed down cautiously to see what was going on. Other Indians appeared silently on foot and soon quite a crowd was watching the activity inside the protective circle that was closing in around the weavers. I decided that must be part of Papa's plan.

I was afraid of what crazy thing Bradford and Benjamin Brownly might think up to spoil it when they got there. Worrying, I turned to look behind me and caught sight of a large squaw coming toward me with a loop stretched open between her hands. She looked straight at me with a toothless grin like a wicked witch and moved closer and closer with that rope in a ring in her hands.

It was like a noose all ready to pop over my head to choke me. She grinned wider and wider as she moved nearer and nearer, and her eyes were as black as the kiss of death.

Right while everyone was paying attention to making baskets that crazy woman was going to kill me! I tried to cry "Papa!" but my throat was paralyzed with fear, and no sound came out.

I buried my head under Papa's arm and squeezed him hard so he could tell that I was frightened. I felt him turn toward the squaw to see what was happening. He laughed and lifted his arm off my face.

"It's all right, Dora," he assured me. "She won't hurt you. She brought you a present."

I peeked out to see what he was talking about and the squaw held out a beautiful string of dried juniper berries and Indian beads. Her black eyes were dancing with pleasure. The toothless old smile was not wicked after all, but warm. I could tell she was as happy about her beads as I was with the ones I had packed in my treasure box.

She put the necklace she was carrying carefully around my neck and stood back to admire the effect.

"Pretty," she said, "Pretty."

"She speaks English," Ed whispered to Papa, and he nodded that he'd noticed.

The squaw pointed at my yellow curls and reached out cautiously to touch one.

"Pretty," she said again. Her face beamed with pleasure.

"Maybe she's never seen golden hair before," Papa said.

I climbed back in the wagon to get the mirror to see how the necklace looked and, while I was there, decided to give my string of beads to the squaw.

I slipped them over her head and held the looking glass in front of her face.

"See," I said, pointing to her image in the glass, "pretty."

I never saw anyone so happy.

"Pretty! Pretty!" she cried, laughing at her reflection.

I handed her the mirror to keep, too, and Papa reached out to squeeze my hand to show me I had done the right thing.

While the braves worked and the others watched, Papa spoke to the squaw in gentle tones. She could understand some words but looked puzzled about others. When she seemed confused, Papa substituted some strange expressions I had never heard before.

He was talking about being friends and someone named Elder Cookson. Must be a relative, I decided. The Indian woman whispered the name to one of the men seated in the circle, and he smiled and nodded.

Just then five more braves came galloping up. The leader, who appeared to be the chief, had a small boy riding in front of him on the horse.

The weavers jumped up to show off their baskets, and all the braves began to speak rapidly in their own language.

Finally, after a lot of talking, the chief spoke to Papa. "Friend," he said and held out his hand. "Friend."

Papa shook it vigorously and repeated, "Friend."

He pulled out his pocketknife, opened and closed it to show how it worked, and handed it to the chief's son, who tried it out and grinned a thank you.

Papa told the chief we needed to be going now, and the Indians stood peacefully by while we drove away.

Ed could hardly wait until we were out of earshot to breathe a big sigh of relief and say, "That was a close call."

"Yup," Papa agreed.

"What kind of words were you speaking to the squaw?"

"Navajo," Papa told him.

"How'd you learn that language?"

"My father taught me to say a few things," Papa replied. "He went on a mission to the Indians when he was young. I didn't know if we'd met up with Utes, Piutes, or Navajos, so I took a chance and when the squaw could understand me, I knew they were Navajos. I was glad, too. Those other tribes are fierce. When I mentioned Elder Cookson, she remembered him and so did some of the braves."

"They liked the baskets," Ed said.

"And the music," I added.

"Yup," Papa agreed.

"How'd you think of it?" Ed asked.

"Inspiration," Papa said, "pure inspiration. Navajos are wonderful weavers, but they make wool rugs mostly and the work is always done by the squaws. When the braves saw a man doing it, I guess that made it all right for them to try it. And Brother Lenstrom's music sort of hypnotized them. Maybe they thought the whole thing was some kind of friendly-white-man ceremony."

"Well, it sure worked," Ed said.

"Yup," Papa said, "it did."

The next day, Sister Owens became so ill that we stopped early. She was a pretty lady with brown eyes, sort of fattish, like Mama. Sister Lenstrom whispered that she was "in a delicate condition," and I took that to mean that she must be kind of sickly.

I was looking forward to exploring with Ed. But Bradford and Benjamin came by, shouting, "Let's hunt horny toads!" and Ed took off with them. I knew they'd torment the girls with the ugly, spiny creatures as soon as they caught some. I was getting sicker and sicker of those Brownly boys. They were nothing but trouble.

Chapter 9

The Tormentors

Bradford was just older than Ed and Benjamin just younger, and they were hanging around him more and more all the time. They didn't like me even a little bit and did everything they could to get rid of me so they could have Ed all to themselves.

If I tried to say anything, they made fun of the way I said it. If I didn't, they pretended I was both deaf *and* dumb and talked about me as if I couldn't hear or else wasn't there at all.

The Brownlys were big boys, and all of us Cooksons were small. They'd move close to Ed with one on one side and one on the other and shoot questions down at him like bullets. The younger one called attention to everything his older brother said by repeating it, and Ed hardly ever had a chance to finish answering what they were asking.

"When's Dumb Dora gonna learn to talk?" Bradford wanted to know.

"Yeah, when?" Benjamin echoed.

"She's learnin'," Ed insisted.

"I thought you said she had her tongue fixed," Bradford went on.

"Yeah, that's what you said."

"She did," Ed agreed.

"Didn't help much, did it?" Bradford said.

"No, it didn't, did it?" Benjamin repeated.

"Takes a long time," Ed told them, "to learn to talk."

"Well, are you the only one who can teach her?" Bradford asked.

"Yeah, the only one?"

"Why can't Caroline do it?"

"Yeah, Caroline could."

"Then you could play some real boys' games without that pesky little sister tagging along."

"Yeah, she's a regular tagalong."

"Why don't you tell her to beat it?" Bradford suggested.

"Beat it!" echoed Benjamin, looking straight at me.

By that time I wanted to beat it forever. I wished the earth would open up and swallow me. I wished I could run into my weeping-willow playhouse and hammer the tree trunk with my fists. I wished we were already in New Mexico in our own house with just our own family.

Most of all, I wished for Ilene. Her exclamation-point fist would have set those Brownly boys straight in a hurry. She'd have let them know that even a girl who can't talk very well has feelings the same as anyone else.

Although I was learning to say more and more words all the time, it was hard. Some of the sounds were easy enough, but some were still impossible. Would I ever be able to talk like other people?

I remembered how happy I had been when the doctor had said he could fix my tongue so I could speak, and how much it had hurt to chew the peppermint stick. That seemed like such a long time ago, and here I was still trying to say words so others could understand them. How long ago was it, really? I counted the finished watermelon scallops on my sampler and added one more. Twenty-four days. Less than a month.

Mama always said, "Time is relative. If you're having fun, it goes fast. If you're not, it drags."

When you're trying to learn to talk, I decided, it goes slower than ever. Tears ran silently down my cheeks.

Late that night when I was still awake feeling sad about things, I could hear Sister Owens moaning in the next wagon. The noise kept up for a long time before her husband scratched at our canvas wagon cover and whispered anxiously to Papa, "What can I do? The baby's coming early and there's no doctor. We expected to be in Clovis in plenty of time."

"Don't worry," Papa said soothingly, "I can help. I've brought all six of ours into the world. One more won't be any trouble."

"Thanks be to God!" Brother Owens cried. "You're an answer to our prayers. I hope you can save the baby this time. We've buried the last two."

A new baby was coming? How exciting! I started to wonder again how God sent babies down from heaven when it was time for them to be born. Did he really use storks to carry them in little bundled-up packages like the pictures showed? I was too small to remember about Ed and Frank, but George and Howie were each wrapped up like that the first time I saw them.

Both times, all the older children had been sleeping over at Grandma Cookson's house, and as soon as we got home in the morning, Papa said, "Mama has a surprise to show you. Go in the bedroom and see what it is."

Each time she was lying in bed holding the new baby cuddled in a cozy blue blanket.

I couldn't figure out how Mr. Owens knew when the baby was coming at all, much less how he could tell it would be early and here instead of in Clovis. And why did he need a doctor? Just in case the stork dropped the bundle from heaven and the baby got hurt? Was that how the other two had died? Was that why Sister Owens sounded so sad already, because she was afraid of what might happen? But what could Papa do to help Brother Owens? What did he mean when he said he'd brought all six of his own into the world?

There were lots of questions I needed to ask as soon as I could talk a little better. I wiggled out from under the wagon to watch the sky for a stork flying over.

For what seemed like forever, I heard the moans getting louder and closer together. I worried about poor Sister Owens who had left two babies behind in the cemetery, and said a prayer of my own for the one that was coming tonight.

"Please, God," I prayed, "let the baby live. And please, please, *please*," I begged, "don't let it be tongue-tied."

I must have dozed off because I didn't see a thing except stars and all of a sudden I heard a new sound, a baby's cry, loud and angry, as if it was afraid of falling or else didn't want to leave heaven.

The next day almost everyone in camp called on Sister Owens and her little girl, Elizabeth Ann, who was wrapped up in a pink blanket and seemed to be happy to be on earth after all. She was tiny but strong and beautiful. Sister Owens let me touch the baby's angel-soft hair, and when she stuck out her tongue I knew it couldn't be tied down.

"Thank you, God." I whispered.

The darling baby girl made me wish for a little sister of my own that I could make pretty clothes for and dress up like a doll. After all those boys, our family needed another girl.

Just before we left the campground, the Indian chief rode up looking for Papa. He had a gift for him—a strange, three-pronged stick shaped like a giant "Y."

"Find water," the chief said.

He held the stick by two of the branches with the third pointed straight ahead and walked around watching the end of it. All at once he tipped it down until it pointed to the ground.

"Water there," the Indian said. "Dig well."

"I understand," Papa said. "It will find the right place to dig for water."

The chief nodded, handed Papa the stick, jumped back on his horse, and rode away.

"What's that?" Mama asked when Papa tucked the branch safely inside the wagon.

"Ever hear of a witching wand?" he asked.

"Nope," Mama said.

"Or a divining rod?"

"Nope."

"Well, sometimes it's called one, sometimes the

other. It's supposed to point to underground water. It might come in handy someday."

"That's just a superstition," Mama scoffed.

It took us nearly two weeks to cut across the southwest corner of Colorado. We went up some and down some and on the flat some, but mostly up, I guess, because one day Papa said we were on the top of the mountains. It didn't seem like we were on the top of any peaks to me. When I looked up at the Wasatch Mountains behind our house back home, I decided that being on top would be like standing on a sharp point and looking down a steep slope in all directions.

Here it was flat and all spread out and no place at all to look down. I should have figured out that was how it would be, though, because I'd been looking at flat-topped mountains instead of sharp, rocky ones for days and days.

Even so, I wondered how Papa could tell we were on the top, so I asked him, "How do you know?"

"Can you see any higher mountains around?" he asked.

I had to admit I couldn't.

"Besides," Papa went on, "I can tell by the elevation. Some of these passes are nearly 8,000 feet high. We're close to the Continental Divide where the water on one side runs down east into the Mississippi River, and on the other side, west to the

Pacific Ocean. That has to be the highest point around."

I didn't exactly understand what he was talking about, but I decided that it was something else I could find out about when I went to school. I filed the words *elevation, Continental Divide, Mississippi River,* and *Pacific Ocean* in my mind so I'd recognize them when the time came.

Sarah Lenstrom and Caroline were spending a lot of time together, and gradually I became friends with Jenny. Jenny had a beautiful shut-eye doll named Samantha with lots of clothes. I took Henrietta and her things out of my chest, and we played house together using Jenny's set of china dishes to have pretend tea parties and play dinners. Time went fast when I spent it with Jenny. First I learned to say "Samantha" and, later, "Jenny."

There were more trees and more streams and more dried grass for the horses and cows to eat in this part of the country. Our scouts often caught fish or killed game for supper. We had deer, elk, wild turkeys, and grouse.

Occasionally we could trade some of the strong-flavored venison to cattle ranchers for milder, more tender cuts of beef. The towns were closer together, too, but they weren't the same as the Latter-day Saint towns in Utah where we were always invited to "sit down and have a bite of supper."

One day didn't seem much different from the day before. With no place to go to church, even Sunday was just the same as any other day. We'll all remember November third, though, the day we spent in Pagosa Springs.

Chapter 10

Pagosa Springs

We'd already traveled a month and weren't much more than halfway to Clovis. The nights had been getting cooler and cooler, cool enough for frost, in fact. I wasn't surprised to see puffy clouds of smoke billowing into the sky as we approached the town late in the afternoon.

As we got closer, however, a peculiar smell, not smoky, was in the air, and Papa sniffed to decide what it was.

"Sulfur," he said. "Must be sulfur springs here. I wonder if *Pagosa* is the Indian word for *sulfur*."

"Don't know," Mama said. "Could be."

"Or maybe *hot*," Papa guessed. "They sure are steaming."

"Hot sulfur springs?" Mama exclaimed. "Like we had just north of Salt Lake in Utah? Oh, Albert, do you think we might . . . "

Mama loved to soak in the hot springs as much she loved to swim in the Great Salt Lake.

"Wouldn't be surprised," Papa answered. "You probably aren't the only one who'd like to have a nice hot bath."

"I would!" I said.

The springs were bubbling out of the ground right next to a scarcely moving stream.

"Well, now," Papa said, "isn't that handy? If the spring water is too hot you can cool it with the river water. No matter what temperature you want, you can mix it up."

Everyone voted to declare a holiday for the next day. We hadn't had one since we left. No one had remembered to mention the day Columbus discovered America. Halloween came and went without any mischievous pranks. Even the Brownly boys hadn't done any damage. That may have been the reason they had so much meanness saved up.

When we woke up the next morning, the whole world looked like fairyland. The warm mist from the springs had frozen into hoar frost around each stalk and stem, on every bush and seed and berry. The dried weed patches looked like tiny fairy forests covered with snow, just the right size for elves and sprites and pixies.

Some of the men rode into town from our camping place to find out where we could swim and located the Great Hot Springs, a public bathhouse.

"Pagosa Springs is a booming metropolis," Papa

told us when he got back. "It has three grocery stores, three meat markets, two hardware stores, a bank, a bakery, a wagon and carriage shop, and even a gent's furnishings store. And a flour mill. How's our flour supply?" he asked Mama.

"Getting low," she replied.

"We'll get a bag," he promised. "I found out that *Pagosa Springs* is an Indian name meaning *healing waters*, so everyone who bathes today should be healthy for a while."

"That'll be a blessing," Mama said.

Right after breakfast, Bradford and Benjamin came by to get Ed. Mama was busy making the bed inside the wagon, and Papa had gone to make sure the horses and cow were safely hobbled.

"Come on, Ed," Bradford announced, "we're goin' fishin'."

"Yeah, fishin'," Benjie echoed.

"Without yer pesky sister," Bradford insisted, staring straight at me, "that can't even talk yet."

"Yeah," Benjie agreed. "Leave Dumb Dora home."

"Thought I'd go swimmin' with everybody else," Ed said.

"*Swimmin'*?" Bradford exploded. "You don't mean sissy swimmin'? In that *warm* water?"

"Not *sissy swimmin'*," Benjie repeated.

"You wanna go swimmin', we'll swim in the river."

"Yeah, the river."

"I don't want . . . " Ed began. He hated cold water.

"He *don't want*," Bradford shouted. "Did you get that, Benjie?"

"Got it," Benjie said. "He *don't want . . .* "

"We'll teach him to *don't want*," Bradford announced.

"Yeah," Benjie agreed, "we'll teach him."

The boys moved closer to Ed, grabbed him under the elbows, and carried him away. They disappeared around a bend downstream, and soon I heard a big splash followed by Ed's loud scream of protest.

He was soaked to the skin and shivering cold when he came back by himself. It's a good thing the Great Hot Springs was there to thaw him out. It seemed to take most of the day before he got warmed up.

"I'm never playing with those big bullies again!" he insisted. I wondered how he was going to avoid it, but he had a plan: keep me with him.

"They hate me!" I objected, thinking they'd be meaner than ever if I was there.

Ed didn't see it that way.

"That's the idea," he said. "They won't want to play with me if they have to play with you, too."

"They'll tease us both," I predicted.

"We'll ignore them," he promised bravely.

"They bigga," I reminded him. (I still couldn't say my r's.)

"Then we'll be smarter," he decided. "Now let's go fishing." He untied his willow pole and pulled out the shovel for digging worms. I found an empty tin can to put them in.

We hadn't seen the Brownly boys since morning when they'd dumped Ed in the river, but just to be sure we didn't meet them, we went in the opposite direction—up the stream. We didn't go far. Getting out of earshot was against Papa's rules.

When we were alone together I tried out my talking. Ed helped me a lot.

"Look at that frog!" he shouted and dropped the things he was carrying as he bounded across the mossy stones to grab it.

"Fwog," I said. "Fwog."

"Not fwog," Ed corrected. "Frog . . . frrrr . . . lift up your tongue like this." He showed me what he meant.

I tried it. "Fwrrrog," I said.

"That's better," he encouraged. "Now keep practicing."

"What a beauty," Ed marveled, examining the frog. "Look how big it is. I wonder how far it can jump."

"Let's twy it," I suggested.

"Try," Ed said, "Trrr . . . try. *Lift up your tongue*!"

I guess the lift-up muscles in my tongue hadn't been used enough to know what to do. Most of the sounds I couldn't say seemed to be made with the end of my tongue in the top of my mouth.

Ed placed the frog on the starting line he'd marked with the fishing pole, then I poked it with a stick to make it jump and marked the ground where it landed so Ed could measure the distance with his feet.

We stayed until nearly dark following the frog as it leaped along, measuring each jump. We didn't notice how late it was getting until we heard Papa calling, and ran to meet him.

"Look at my frog, Papa," Ed said.

"That's a fine one, all right," Papa agreed.

"Can I keep it?" Ed coaxed. "Can I?"

"No, Son," Papa said. "You'd better leave it here."

"But I need a pet," Ed argued.

Papa shook his head. "It would only die if you took it."

"No it wouldn't," Ed insisted. "I'll put it in a bucket of water. And feed it. And . . . "

"A bucket of water isn't the same as a stream. This is where it belongs."

"Please, Papa."

"No, Ed. Now put it down and I'll tell you a story on the way back." Papa reached for my hand.

"What about?" Ed asked.

"About a frog."

"A true story?"

"Absolutely."

Papa's stories were usually worth listening to. Ed put his pet in a cozy spot by the stream, picked up the fishing pole, and took hold of Papa's other hand. The three of us began to walk toward camp.

"What's the story?" Ed wanted to know.

"How butter was discovered."

"You said it was about a frog."

"So it is. You see, a long time ago a frog jumped into a bowl of cream that was left by a dairy maid to keep cool at the edge of a stream. Her name was Betty."

"Mama?" I asked.

"No," Papa replied, "a different Betty. The frog paddled around all night trying to get out, and when Betty came the next morning to get the cream, it had been turned to butter."

"Was the frog still in it?"

"I don't remember that, but since there was no cream to spread on the bread, the dairy maid used the butter instead. She sprinkled it, as usual, with a dash of salt and a spoonful of sugar. She expected to be scolded for being careless enough to leave the cover off the bowl, but everyone liked the new spread even better than cream.

" 'Betty, get that better spread,' her mistress said.

When the first batch was gone, she asked her to make more."

"How did she know how unless she'd found the frog?" Ed asked.

"I guess maybe she did," Papa decided, "or else she figured it out. Anyway, she made it. They called it 'Betty's better spread' until someone changed the name to butter."

"Oh, Papa," Ed said, "you just made up that story."

"Me? Make up a story?" Papa asked as if he were surprised that anyone could think such a thing. "I'd never do that, would I?"

We couldn't tell if he had or not.

By then we were back by the wagon smelling the cutthroat trout Mama had sizzling in the frying pan. Afterward there was a camp-fire program ending with evening prayer. Then the children were put to bed under the wagons. Soon Brother Lenstrom's fiddle began its tune, and the grown-ups were moving their feet to the music. While we watched the dancing, I tried out the "fr" sound with my tongue.

"F-f-fr-fr-frrog-frog," I whispered to Ed.

"That's good, Dora," he said. "Very good."

The next morning the ladies decided to have wash day while they had such nice hot water. Papa thought the sulfur might make the clothes smell funny, but Mama promised to rinse them enough to get rid of the odor.

He started filling our wash barrel with the steaming water, and Mama added a bar of homemade lye soap and tossed the dirty clothes in to jostle around as the wagons bounced along.

By the time the day's journey was over, the clothes would be clean. Then we'd rinse, wring, and hang them up on ropes stretched between the trees. We always camped early on wash day to make sure the clothes had plenty of time to dry—and by a stream so we'd have plenty of rinse water. All the children had some extra hours to play, too, after their chores were done.

That day the girls were anxious to get on with the jacks tournament. Sarah Lenstrom had challenged all the others to a contest for the championship. She had a real leather bag to keep her ball and jacks in, and everyone knew she would win because she almost never missed. She could play just as well with her left hand as her right, so if one got tired, she just switched to the other.

Still, Caroline was a good player, too, and could usually give Sarah a run for her money. She could separate two jacks that were nearly touching, grabbing the one without even stirring the other, and was really fast at double eggs-in-a-basket. The only smooth surface they could find to play on was Sister Lenstrom's breadboard. They kept at it so long that all their fingernails were worn down to the quick on the side that brushed against the wood to pick up the jacks.

Wash day was a busy time, and we all had to help out more than usual. While Papa finished filling the barrel with the smelly water, Mama assigned the chores.

"Caroline, you and Frank take care of the chickens," she instructed. "Make sure they're fed and watered and don't let any of them get lost when you turn them out to run. Don't spend so much time petting that rooster that you forget the hens.

"Dora, I'll need you to watch George and Howie while I do the washing, and Ed, you can churn the butter."

"I hate to churn butter," Ed objected. "Let Caroline do it."

"She has her own jobs," Mama told him.

"Butter churning is girls' work," he insisted.

"Don't argue with me, young man," Mama said in her I-won't-put-up-with-any-nonsense voice. "Half an hour's work isn't worth making such a fuss about. You can do it while we ride along, and it will be all done by the time we stop. We need it for supper." Just then I saw the look come into Ed's eyes that meant he had an idea, and I knew what it was because I had it, too.

Chapter 11

Churning the Butter

Ed jerked his head at me in a way that said "come on" and grabbed a bar of soap and a towel, and we ran off in the direction of the stream.

"Where are you two going?" Mama called.

Ed shouted, "To wash our hands."

"You lie," I reminded him when we stopped by the creek.

"No I didn't," he replied, "we'll wash our hands. And the word is lie*d*. *D-D-D* on the end. Lift up your tongue and then drop it down to let the air out."

Lift up my tongue! I should have known that was the problem. It always was. Making each sound was a different combination of moving my tongue and my lips and making the air go past. How come it was so easy for babies and so hard for me? I tried to do what Ed described.

The frog hadn't warmed up enough to move around yet, so it was still where we had left it the night before.

Ed started to lather it with the soap, and it slipped out of his hands. He picked up the slick frog again, and I gave him my "what-are-you-doing?" look. He said, "Getting it clean enough."

After he washed, rinsed, and dried the frog, Ed put it inside his shirt. We scrubbed our hands to make us honest and stayed by the stream cutting willows until the company was ready to leave. It's a good thing we did, because we found the shovel Ed had dropped the day before when he first caught the frog. At the last minute, we ran and jumped in the back of the wagon.

Mama rode in front with Papa, holding George on her lap. Frank and Caroline were spending the day with the Lenstroms and Howie was asleep in the wagon bed. We had the whole place to ourselves.

Ed plopped the frog in the butter churn, and we settled down for a lazy ride. It was a good thing we had the kind of churn we did. One like the Lenstroms' with a paddle wheel turned by a handle had too many jumping-out-to-rest places where a frog could sit without even being in the cream. Ours was like a small keg turned on its side that rocked back and forth like a cradle and sloshed the cream into butter. The frog had to swim or drown.

We reached over the tailgate, dragging our willows in the dust to make patterned trails behind us. After a while Ed decided to show me how to make willow whistles, but the bark was dry and cracked and wouldn't slip off the way it was supposed to.

"Wrong time of year, I guess," he said.

Several times we peeked into the churn where the frog was still swimming around, but there was no sign of butter. Ed started trying to teach me to say "Betty's better spread," and we forgot about everything else until the wagon stopped for our noon meal.

As soon as we climbed out, Mama asked, "Did the butter come yet?"

"Not yet," Ed told her.

"Have you been working at it or just daydreaming?" Mama asked.

"Yeah," Ed said without answering which.

"Well, you'd better get it done before supper," she said sternly, "or else you'll be in trouble."

Papa then told her the frog story, and she said, "Now, Albert, don't go giving those children any crazy ideas. It would be just like Ed and Dora to try that out."

She shook her finger at us. "And don't you *dare*!" she warned.

Ed and I both expected Mama to check in the churn that very minute to see if we were already guilty, but, luckily, she was too busy fixing the food. We didn't dare look at each other for fear she would notice and get even more suspicious. We stayed close to the wagon, however, watching and waiting anxiously for a chance to get that frog out of the cream before she found it. After we did, Ed would be glad to make the butter the way he was supposed to.

When we finished eating, we jumped quickly into the back of the wagon, and Ed heaved a big sigh of relief as if he'd been holding his breath for a very long time. "That was close," he whispered. I nodded.

Just then Caroline climbed in, followed by Frank. They had decided they wanted to ride in our wagon now and settled down right next to the churn.

I stared at Ed with my *what-do-we-do-now* look, and he shrugged his *I-don't-know* answer.

I knew he didn't want to start rocking the churn as fast as we usually did for fear he'd bang the frog against the sides and kill it or maybe even mash it up, but we both knew he had to have some butter in time for supper.

"You'd better start churning," Caroline reminded Ed in a bossy tone of voice.

"I will," he agreed, but he didn't move a muscle to do it.

"I'm gonna tell Mama," Caroline threatened.

Ed reached for the handle and moved it back and forth very slowly.

"You'll never get butter that way," Caroline told him.

"Mind your own business!" Ed exploded. "You do your work and I'll do mine."

"Well, don't say I didn't warn you," Caroline shot back. "See if I care if you get a whipping." She tossed her head, opened the book she'd borrowed from Sarah Lenstrom, and began to read.

Frank soon fell asleep, and Ed leaned back, yawned loudly, and closed his eyes. I could tell from the way he looked at me and then at Caroline that he was hoping to make her sleepy, too, and that I was supposed to wake him up if she dozed off. No such luck. Caroline was as wide awake as her pet rooster at daybreak.

I could feel my own eyes getting heavy, but I knew I had to watch for a chance to take care of that frog, so I fought to stay awake. I decided to work on the sampler and took it carefully from the chest. I counted the finished melon slices. Thirty-two. Twelve more to go and the border would be finished. Would we be in Clovis by then? I hoped so.

I started thinking about talking plain enough to go to school in New Mexico. Maybe the sampler could tell about that. If I put the maze in the middle, in black outline stitch . . . and the crooked, slammed door (brown) in the top left corner . . . down at the bottom, like the happily-ever-after ending of a story, could be an open door—a nice, clean, painted-white door—the one to the schoolroom.

In between, I could make pictures of the things that happened on the trip: jumping rope . . . playing jacks . . . Indians weaving baskets . . . and crossing t h e r i v . . . .

The next thing I knew Papa was calling "Whoa!" to the horses, and the wagon was slowing down to a stop. The frog was still in the churn, the butter wasn't done, and Ed was asleep. The sun was still high in the sky.

Then I remembered that it was wash day, and we were stopping early. The boys woke up, and I helped Frank climb down over the tailgate.

Caroline put a marker in her book and slammed it shut. She stepped past Ed and me and said, "I'm going to tell Mama you didn't make the butter."

Ed stuck his tongue out at her, grabbed the churn handle, and yelled after her, "I'm doing it now."

As soon as she was out of sight, he lifted the lid to rescue the frog. It sat high on top of the island of butter it had whipped up: a green frog with black spots on creamy butter, a perfect picture for my sampler.

"Butter," I said. "Frog."

Ed grabbed it and tucked it inside his shirt in one quick movement. He closed the lid of the churn and jumped down from the wagon with me right behind him.

"Butter's done," he called to Mama.

"Good boy!" she called back. "I knew you could do it."

"I don't believe it," Caroline said and looked to see. "It must have churned itself," she muttered. "Ed didn't do it."

We took off for the stream as fast as we could go to turn the frog loose and to laugh at our luck, and then hurried back for me to tend George and Howie while Mama finished the washing.

Neither one of us ever told how the butter was churned that day, and of course I couldn't give our secret away by putting it on the sampler. Papa didn't tell, either. But I knew he knew. Every time he reached for the butter dish, he winked at me.

The Brownly boys came by for Ed just as if nothing had happened the day before. They had a collection to show him.

"Boiled frogs," Bradford said, pulling a pie plate from behind him. It was piled high with dead frogs.

"Yeah," Benjie repeated, "boiled."

"That's what we found when we went fishin'," Bradford explained, "in the boiling hot bug holes by the river. They just jumped in and cooked themselves."

"Jumped and cooked," Benjie repeated.

I could tell by the way Ed looked at me that he was glad we'd saved one frog from jumping into a hot spring.

The next day Papa announced that we were in New Mexico. We must be nearly there, I thought. But Papa showed me the map, and I could tell it was still farther than all the way we had come across Colorado.

We traveled gradually downhill along the river, making as much distance in a day as we could. Trees were getting farther and farther apart except along the stream, where the cottonwoods were thick.

Santa Fe was by far the biggest city we'd seen, but we were too anxious to be on our way to stop very long to look it over. We noticed that all of the buildings were the color of dirt and all of the corners were rounded instead of square.

"Made of adobe clay," Papa explained.

We stopped at one store to buy a hundred-pound bag of cornmeal, and at another to replace Papa's pocketknife. Mama fell in love with some pretty striped and knobby gourds, and Papa got her a couple.

"You can save the seeds and grow your own," he told her.

I needed more green embroidery thread, and Caroline begged for a leather bag like Sarah's to carry her jacks in.

Then we were on our way again. I wonder if we'd have been so eager to leave Santa Fe behind if we had known how hard the journey ahead would be.

Chapter 12

Thanksgiving

All the trees were disappearing and, for the first time, we saw cactus scattered among the sparse, brushy growth. The hills gave way to flat land, and mile after mile, day after dreary day, we traveled through dry, desert wasteland.

Papa's predicted travel time of five or six weeks was all used up, and still we were not close to Clovis. The watermelon border of forty-four smiles was finished all around my sampler, but we had farther yet to go. I drew more slices in my notebook to keep track of the number of days, but I made them upside down, like frowns.

It was time to finish the pattern for the inside of the frame to tell the story of the trip, but I didn't have enough energy to do it. My notebook was full of drawings and someday I would arrange them in the right order. But not yet.

Once I had mastered "l" and "r," I learned to say

anything I needed to. I had been storing words in my head for so many years that I had plenty of things I was waiting to say. The only problem was that I often repeated the easy beginning sound of a word while I concentrated on forming the more difficult parts that followed. The result was that I stuttered.

"Don't worry," Mama encouraged. "You'll soon stop that."

I was tired of the effort. I was tired of the trip, tired of the desert, tired of everything. Would I ever again see the green valleys and beautiful jagged mountain peaks we'd left behind in Utah?

Where were the miles and miles of watermelon patches I was expecting? Even in November there should be some withered vines and rotting fruit left in the fields. But there weren't even any fields. Only dry, sandy desert with a few spiky cactus.

What lived here besides lizards and horny toads? We saw no people. No horses. No cows or chickens. We had more of all of those in our wagon train than we saw in a week of riding in New Mexico.

Each night Papa marked a short line on the map indicating the distance of the day's travel. Clovis, marked with a star, seemed as far away as the stars in the sky.

Supplies were getting low, fresh meat was impossible to find, and we ate the chickens one by one.

"I'm glad you thought to bring them," Papa told Mama.

Finally, on the forty-ninth day after leaving Murray, we came to Fort Sumner, where the land office was. We arrived on a Sunday night and camped outside of town. Early the next morning our wagons were pulled up in front of the government building to take care of the necessary business as soon as possible.

Brother Talbot came outside to welcome us and introduced himself to each family in turn.

"I thought you'd never get here," he said to Papa.

"We wondered, too," Papa told him.

"The Church members are anxious to see you and they have their welcome mats out," Brother Talbot said. "I have the papers all ready for you to sign. Your place is the farthest away from Clovis. Almost to Texico, in fact. Brother Williamson lives close by, and he'll show you where your piece is."

"How do I find him?" Papa asked.

Brother Talbot laughed. "Ask anyone in Clovis," he said. "By the way, the Hoyts haven't moved out of the house yet, so he's found a temporary place for you to stay."

"That's fine," Papa said. "How much farther is it?"

"About sixty miles to Clovis," Brother Talbot said, "seventy to Texico."

"Seventy miles!" Mama exclaimed. "That'll take four more days."

"Just about," Mr. Talbot agreed. "You'll have to hurry to get there in time to have Thanksgiving dinner with the Williamsons."

Thanksgiving dinner? No one had mentioned that this was the week for Thanksgiving.

I had almost forgotten what it was like to be invited to "sit down and have a bite to eat." But I remembered in a hurry and started getting hungry right away.

"That's an appropriate day to arrive," Papa said. "We'll have plenty to be thankful for."

"The Clovis Branch will be thankful for so many new members, too," Brother Talbot said. "You'll fill up that old house clear to the rafters."

He told us how to find the Sunday meeting place, and with great eagerness, we set out on the last leg of the journey to our new home.

I was so anxious to get there that it seemed like the longest part of the trip. Why did it seem to take everyone so long to get going in the morning? Why did the horses move so slowly and stop so often to eat? Why did it get dark before we had a chance to travel very far?

When we finally neared Clovis, three days later, the wagons pulled off in different directions, one by one, as they got close to the homesteads they were headed for.

"See you at church," we'd call as they left.

I had never seen such flat land. Not a sign of a rise anywhere. And colored reddish brown, not black like Holladay dirt. It looked like God had rolled out a big batch of gingerbread dough with a giant rolling pin, I decided, sprinkled it with cinnamon, and left it in the sun to bake. Sometimes dust devils rose up like puffs of powdered spice, and I could imagine the snappy fragrance.

The Lenstroms were still with us after we'd passed through the town of Clovis, which meant that their place would be closer to ours than any of the other traveling families.

"That's something else to be thankful for," Papa said. "We can give each other a hand now and then."

"And go for a v-visit," I added, "to play with Jenny and Sarah."

"How about staying tonight?" Papa asked.

"Yes, yes!" I said.

Papa helped the Lenstroms locate their homestead, and we camped there till morning, when we started out looking for the Williamsons.

As Brother Talbot had predicted, the first person we asked knew where they lived. "Just four more miles along the road to Texico."

Sister Williamson had a huge turkey roasted golden brown in the oven for Thanksgiving dinner.

"My, my," she greeted us, "what a nice lot of helpers. As soon as we set the table, mash the potatoes, and whip the cream, we'll be ready to eat."

It wasn't quite that quick to dinnertime, but once we sat down we all ate as if we'd been saving our appetites for a month. It had been longer than that since we'd last eaten in a house.

After the meal was over, Papa said, "How would you like to show us to our new home?"

"You bet," Brother Williamson agreed, standing up. "I'll saddle the horse and ride right over there with you."

When we climbed into our wagon, Papa was smiling. "We're almost there," he said, "to the place of our dreams."

Chapter 13

Dream or Nightmare?

We rode for a quite a while, farther and farther from Clovis.

Mama said, "We're getting a long ways from the church."

"Yes, we are," Papa agreed. "Must be six or eight miles by now."

Still we drove on. We passed a few farms where cultivated land had been harvested and only stubble remained. Some fields had been plowed. Most of the land was still wild, covered with the same scrawny brush and round clumps of spiky cactus that we'd been seeing for days and days. Some of the clumps had fat, dry stems poking up in the middle holding up big brown seed pods.

The route changed direction several times, and it was clear that, without Brother Williamson's help, we would have had difficulty finding the piece we were looking for.

"There's your closest store," Brother Williamson said, pointing to a two-story building.

Papa read the name: "Younger's General Merchandise."

"The family lives above the store," Brother Williamson explained. "That's the school across the street."

The school? I jerked my head around in a hurry to see a small wooden building that looked nearly new. It hadn't even been painted yet.

It couldn't be more than one large room, I decided. I wondered how a whole school could fit into such a small place and was anxious to find out. I paid close attention to all the turns in the road after that so I'd know how to get back there.

The sun was getting low in the west when we first saw our homestead. It certainly didn't look like the lush, green, covered-with-watermelons Garden of Eden that I was expecting. I don't know what had made me think our place was going to be any different from all the other farms around, but somehow I had.

Brother Williamson slowed his horse and pointed to a stick with a red rag tied to it.

"Your property begins right there at that stake," he told Papa, "and extends half a mile east, south, west, then north to make a square."

Papa looked over the parcel of land. "Sure is

level," he said. "No trees to clear off. Not much here but weeds and cactus."

"It's a good piece," Brother Williamson assured him. "Needs a little work, is all."

Papa pulled on the reins to stop the horses and jumped down from the wagon. Caroline, Ed, and I climbed out after him. He kicked the cinnamon-colored soil with his boot, picked up a handful, and let it trickle through his fingers.

"Good sandy loam," he said. "Nothing better for growing crops." He looked toward some low, sandy hills in the distance.

"Don't see any mountains," he said. "Where does the water come from? I'm used to having streams pouring out of every canyon."

Brother Williamson laughed. "No canyons here," he said. "Or streams either. You have to depend on the rain. But don't worry, there's always enough for good crops."

"What about drinking water?"

"Most people have wells," Brother Williamson said with a strange tone in his voice that made me wonder if there was something he didn't want to tell Papa.

"What happens if there's a drought?"

"Dries up," Brother Williamson said. "Same as anyplace."

"What do people grow around here?"

"Corn mostly. Sweet corn and maize, and sorghum-type crops like milo, kafir, and broom corn. You can sell all the broom corn you can grow to the factory over in Texico, and there's nothing better than milo and maize to feed livestock."

Papa walked along slowly, leading the horses and sizing up the property.

"Where's the house?" Papa asked.

"Down around the corner," Brother Williamson said.

"Get in, children," Papa instructed us, "and we'll drive to it."

Soon after we turned the bend in the road, we came to two extremely tall upright posts set far enough apart for a gate, but there was none. The only sign of a fence was a roll of rusted barbed wire leaning against one of the posts.

"There it is," Brother Williamson said, pointing to an unpainted shack almost hidden in a tangle of weeds. "It's not very big. You'll have to add on. The Hoyts should be back from Texas in a week or so to pick up their things. Until then, you can start on the barn. There's a pile of lumber behind the house."

"There's no hurry for a barn in this warm country, is there?" Papa asked.

Brother Williamson laughed so hard he almost fell off his horse. "Where do you think you are?" he asked. "In Florida? Any day now we'll get a cold wind from the north, and you'll think you've moved to Alaska. The barn better be tight or it will be full of sand. And it better be strong or it will go down in the wind.

"Quick as a wink the wind can change from north to south, warm everything up, and melt the snow."

"Snow?" Papa, Caroline, Ed, and I all asked at once.

"Oh, not much," he said, "but some every year. The altitude here is over 4,000 feet, not much different from Salt Lake Valley. We have a long, hot growing season, but we have a frosty winter."

I couldn't believe it. Was that dirty-looking wreck of a house in the middle of a weed patch in another cold climate the answer to Mama's and Papa's prayers? It seemed like their dream had turned into a nightmare. I wanted to cry. What lay ahead for us? Would all our rosy plans to have a place of our own be just a repeat of the struggle we'd had in Utah—long days of hard work and never enough money? I had an empty, frightened feeling in the pit of my stomach.

Caroline could tell how awful I felt. She put an arm around me and whispered, "Don't worry, Dora, Papa will build us a new house and let us have that one to play in."

"I hope we c-can c-c-clean it up," I choked.

Mama was silent. Her lips were pressed together in a thin, tight line.

"Where are our temporary living quarters?" Papa asked, all of a sudden in a big hurry to go.

"It's only a dugout," Brother Williamson apologized, "but it's not too far away, and it's cozy."

He led us another mile or two toward the sand hills to a shabby shanty that looked even worse than the house. It wasn't much bigger than the wagon. A low roof sloped down to the ground on two sides. At one end was a door and dirt steps leading down to a room that had been dug out of the ground. A small window in the opposite end gave the only light.

Brother Williamson offered to help Papa and Ed move things in before he went back home, but all Mama wanted unloaded was the stove.

"I don't want anything else in that dingy cave," she insisted after he left, "until I've cleaned out every corner."

There was bread and warm milk from the cow for anyone who wasn't still full of turkey, and we prepared to sleep out under the stars again, but not until after we'd had a family prayer to say thanks for our safe arrival.

Even while Papa was saying the words, I wondered what there was to be thankful for in this forsaken wilderness of weeds and cactus.

The next morning Papa said another prayer of

thanks that we were going to have our own place at last, and when I saw the look of trust that Mama gave him, I knew everything was going to be all right after all, no matter how much work it cost us.

My worries of the night before seemed to melt away in the cheerful morning sunshine, and I made up my mind to be as much help as I could.

Papa took Ed and me with him to look over our land, leaving Caroline and Frank to help Mama clean out the dugout and move things in.

We walked all around and across our quarter section. One spot wasn't much different from another. It was all flat, sandy, and treeless. In his mind Papa had already laid out the farm into orchard, pasture, crop land, vegetable garden, and corral. He showed Ed and me where each was to be.

"Sure is different from Utah," Papa said. "No rocks, no mountains, no trees, and no irrigation ditches. Not even any creeks with water. A bad drought could wipe out a crop."

My stomach felt hollow again.

Behind the house, almost buried by weeds, we found a pile of lumber that had been there a long time.

"For the barn," Papa said.

Every once in a while we came upon deep holes that had been dug in the sandy soil, and finally Ed asked what they were for.

"I've been trying to figure that out," Papa said, "and I've about decided they're probably places where the Hoyts tried to dig wells."

"Why so many?" I asked.

"Couldn't quit till they found water," Papa explained.

"Did they ever find it?" Ed wanted to know.

"No," Papa said in a strange tone, "I don't believe they did. It seems to me that Brother Talbot said they got tired of hauling water to drink, and I thought they were just too lazy to dig a well, but it looks as if . . . " Papa got a funny expression on his face and didn't finish the sentence for a long time.

Finally he said, "They probably didn't dig deep enough."

"P-Pretty deep," I said, peering down into one of the holes.

"But not deep enough," Papa repeated.

"What if *we* can't find water?" Ed asked.

"We'll find it," Papa promised us. I could tell he wasn't as convinced as he tried to sound. "It *has* to be here," he insisted fiercely. The scared, empty feeling in my stomach spread until it pushed my heart into a lump in my throat. Papa's bubbly excitement had gone flat like bread that has risen too high.

We headed slowly and silently back toward the dugout. Shortly before we arrived, he stopped and spoke to us.

"I don't want your mama worrying about water," he said. "Do you understand?"

"Yeah," Ed replied. "I won't say anything."

"Dora?"

I nodded. I could feel my eyes get wet and my chin start to shake.

Papa grabbed me in a hug. "I don't want you worrying about it either," he said. "God sent us down here to this place, and he knows we have to have water."

"Maybe the Indian's stick can find it," Ed suggested.

"I'm counting on that," Papa said.

We arrived at the dugout just in time for the noon meal. It seemed like a different place than we'd left four hours before. Already Mama and Caroline had it looking and smelling like home. They'd cleaned up, found places for everything, figured out where everyone would sleep, and had dinner all ready.

"You're a wonder, hon'," Papa told Mama and gave her a kiss. "I'll build us a table and chairs first chance I get."

"No place to put them till we get in the house," Mama told him as she passed the sandwiches around. "We'll have to camp out for a while longer."

We ate outside in the sunshine, sitting on the overall quilt Caroline had spread out.

After dinner Papa and Ed hooked up the stovepipe and put it through a hole in the roof.

"All ready to use," Papa told Mama.

"Except for some fuel," she said. "There's no wood around here to burn, except packing boxes and barrels."

"There's some coal up by the house," Papa said. "I'll bring you some."

He picked up the shovel.

"We found a few holes I need to fill up before George and Howie fall in," he told Mama. "Come on, Ed and Dora." He nodded at the dry stick the Indian had given him, and I knew that meant to bring it. I remembered that Mama didn't believe in its magic powers.

When we walked onto our piece of land, Papa handed the shovel to Ed and reached for the stick. "Let's see that divining rod," he said to me with a wink. "It should be thirsty enough by now to find water. There's no time like the present to solve a problem."

"The convenient place for a well," he said as we walked past the sagging shack, "is behind the house. We'll look here first."

"No holes here," Ed observed. "I wonder why."

"Probably filled them up," Papa reasoned, "this close to the house."

Holding the branch horizontal to the earth with

one prong in each hand and the other pointing straight ahead, Papa walked slowly around the area where he hoped to have a well. Nothing happened. He tried again, shaking his head.

He moved gradually outward in a bigger and bigger circle, giving special attention to the places where digging had already been started. After he gave up on an empty hole, we all took turns shoveling in the light, sandy soil to fill it.

When dusk came, Papa poked the stick in the ground to mark the place to begin looking for water the next day, and we started back. His shoulders were sagging more than usual. I put a pretend smile on my face so Mama wouldn't figure out that maybe our Garden of Eden was really a waterless wilderness.

Chapter 14

Only God Knows

The next day Papa tried the water stick again in a new part of the property and filled some more of the deep, dry wells. Then he marked the edges of the barn, pulled the weeds away from the woodpile, and began building. Ed and I held the boards while he nailed them together. We saved the scraps to burn in the stove.

I knew that building the barn was Papa's excuse for not digging the well first. As long as we were in the dugout, we had to haul water anyway, so it didn't really matter—yet.

Mama had noticed that Papa wasn't his usual happy self, however. "You look peaked," she said. "You're working too hard."

"Well, tomorrow's a day of rest," he told her. "We'll go in to Clovis to church."

I unpacked my white Bible and took it with me. It was good to be in Sunday School again and to see all the people we'd traveled with. The meetinghouse really was a house, a big one with enough rooms for Sunday School classes. It was crowded.

On the way home, we stopped at the Lenstroms' to have dinner and fill the water barrels. Lenstroms' house wasn't very big, either, but it was better than ours.

"I'll have it fixed up in no time," Brother Lenstrom said. He was a first-class carpenter, and Papa agreed to build him a fireplace in exchange for some work on our house.

Every day, no matter what else he did, Papa went out with the divining rod to try to locate the place for a well. He didn't say anything about it, but I could tell that he was getting more and more worried.

"This is getting to be a nuisance," Mama complained every time she ran out of water. "When are you going to dig a well?"

"Pretty soon," Papa promised, warning me with a look not to mention the reason he hadn't done it yet.

After a week of useless off-and-on searching, we spent an entire afternoon walking around the property trying to find water. The stick continued to point straight ahead without the slightest dip toward the ground.

"Wh-wh-where *is* that w-water?" I finally cried out.

"Only God knows," Papa said with a weary sigh. "I surely don't."

"Then wh-why don't you ask him?" I said softly.

"What did you say?"

"I said if only G-G-God knows, why don't you ask him?"

"Of course!" Papa agreed. "That's the problem! What on earth is the matter with me, anyway? I've depended so much on that Indian stick that I forgot all about praying. I purposely didn't mention it to God at home for fear I'd worry Mama."

We knelt down right where we were, and Papa poured out his heart to God as if he were talking to a friend. I opened my eyes for a peek to see if maybe God wasn't floating right there in the air above us waiting to give his answer.

When we stood up again, Papa was like a different man. He held the stick as if it were a magic wand and started off like he knew just where he had to go. Nothing had happened by supper time, though.

"Maybe G-God's not going to answer your p-prayer," I worried.

"Oh yes he is!" Papa insisted. "He may try our faith a while longer, but we're going to find water. I know it. I could feel the way the stick will pull down right while I was praying."

"Could you tell where?" I asked, getting to the important point.

"Nope," he told me, "I couldn't. We'll have to keep looking." He poked the rod in the ground at the edge of the lane to the house, and we started back to the dugout.

In the morning, Papa saw smoke coming out of the Hoyts' chimney, so he knew they were back. We went over to find out when they were moving. On the way, Papa picked up the witching wand.

Suddenly he stopped, took the stick in both hands, and held it out in front of him. It tipped toward the ground.

"Look at that, Dora," he said. "I think we've found water."

"Are you f-fooling me?" I asked.

"No," Papa insisted. "All of a sudden I had this feeling that I was supposed to pay attention. Then something pulled the stick down. I didn't even have it pointed."

"B-But that's the m-middle of the road," I said. "You can't dig . . ."

"Oh, can't I?" Papa exclaimed gleefully. "I can jolly well dig anywhere there's water. We can move the road. We may even have to move the house." Papa sounded as if he felt strong enough to do it with his bare hands.

"I don't know why I never tried out here before," he said.

"You didn't ask before," I reminded him.

"You're right," he agreed. "I never would have thought of it myself, it seems like such a funny place to put up a water tank."

"Water tank?"

"Yes, to store the water."

Papa said the word *water* like he was mentioning gold. He was so happy he danced up to the Hoyts' door and knocked on it with a lively rat-a-tat-tat. He found out that they would be gone the next day and went to work with new energy to put the finishing touches on the barn.

By evening the animals were cozy inside the stable, and there was a pile of soft hay in the loft above. Ed and I begged to sleep there.

"Not until we move into the house," Papa said. "It's too far away from the rest of the family now."

That night when Papa prayed, "Thank you, God, for the successful events of this day," I knew that he was talking about finding water. I don't know what Mama thought he meant.

The next day, Ed, Caroline, Frank, and I were sitting in the doorway of the barn loft, watching the Hotys pack up their wagon.

"I wish they'd hurry and go so we can move in," Ed said.

"I wonder if they'll leave anything," Caroline said.

"P-p-probably not," I predicted.

"The Lenstroms found all sorts of good things left in their house," Caroline reminded us.

"Like what?" I asked.

"A table and some fruit bottles."

"And a pretty good harness in the barn," Frank put in.

"Don't forget the stove," Ed added. "They left a good stove."

"The oven has to be propped shut with a stick of wood," Caroline mentioned, "or it falls down."

"It's still good," Ed insisted.

By the time the Hoyts finished putting all their things into the wagon and finally started out the gate, it didn't seem possible that anything could be left in the house. We scrambled down the loft ladder and ran to look inside, anyway. There was just a single room and it was completely empty except for one very important thing.

"A high chair!" Caroline exclaimed. "Look at that. Howie can have a high chair."

"That should keep him out of mischief at mealtime," Ed said.

"And while Mama cooks," Frank added.

"I wish they'd left a table," Caroline said. "That's what we really need. And some more chairs."

"Papa said he'd m-make some," I reminded her, "after we m-move in."

Mama was already coming through the door with

her mop bucket full of sudsy water, and she and Caroline started scrubbing down the walls while the rest of us went back to the dugout to move our things.

While Mama was deciding where everything went, Ed said, "I get to sleep in the barn."

"Me too," I insisted.

"Nothing doing," Mama warned. "The barn's for animals, not children."

"Papa promised," Ed told her.

"It's all right, hon'," Papa told Mama. "The loft's clean and warm and close enough that we could hear them call if they needed us."

"Well, even such a big room can get pretty crowded," Mama agreed, "with eight people living and eating and sleeping in it."

"Please, Mama," Ed coaxed.

"P-please," I echoed.

"I guess it won't hurt to try it," Mama conceded, and we started out the door with some of our things.

George grabbed onto my legs and shouted, "I wanna sleep with Dora! I wanna sleep with Dora."

"Let him come, Mama," I said. "I'll t-take c-care of him."

"Watch him, then, so he doesn't fall down the ladder," she cautioned.

"I don't fall down ladders," George said in a huff. "I climb down."

"That's good," Mama told him. "Then you won't get hurt."

Ed and I took a load of bedding to the barn, and I carried up my treasure chest.

Papa couldn't wait to start digging the well. He checked the location one more time with the witching wand and began shoveling dirt like he was expecting to find gold. He was just getting a good start when Mama walked down from the house and said, "You're not putting the well there, are you?"

"Yup," Papa said, "right here."

"In the middle of the road?" Mama couldn't believe it. "In the front yard?"

"Yup."

"Why? It doesn't make any sense."

"It does if you've been through what I've been through to find water." Then he told her.

"I hope you've found it now," Mama said as if she didn't believe God would use a witching wand to show Papa where the water was.

"Me too," Papa agreed, and kept on digging.

Chapter 15

Christmas in New Mexico

Papa sent Ed and me to get some boards to support the sides of the well so they wouldn't cave in. When he got down so deep he couldn't throw the dirt out, he rigged up a bucket on a pulley. We wound it up, emptied the dirt out, and sent it back down for Papa to fill again.

Day after day for nearly a week, he shoveled deeper and deeper. The hole was three times as tall as Papa was, and still there was no water. His shoulders began to sag again, but he kept on digging.

One day he called up to me, "The ground's too hard for the shovel; send the pickax down in the bucket."

Slowly he chipped through a foot or two of shaley rock. Underneath it the ground was moist.

"Hadn't better dig any deeper," he said when he climbed up out of the hole. "Water might come in fast enough to drown me before I could get out. I've heard some mighty scary stories about that. We'll just wait a while and see what happens."

Then he picked up the saw and said, "Who wants to go with me to look for a Christmas tree?"

"I do!" Ed shouted.

"M-me, too," I declared.

"I want to go," Frank insisted.

"Where can you find a Christmas tree?" Mama asked. "I haven't seen any pine trees growing around here. Or any trees, for that matter."

"Don't know," Papa said. "Maybe we'll have to use a cactus."

"A cactus Christmas tree?" Frank sounded disappointed.

"Why not?" Papa asked. "Think how pretty it would be with paper chains and popcorn strings hanging from the prickles."

"I guess so," Frank conceded.

"I'll pop the corn while you're gone," Mama offered. "We'll string it when you get back."

We tramped around in the warm sunshine trying to imagine that it was winter and that Christmas was nearly here. It seemed more like April than December.

"As soon as you see a good Christmas tree," Papa instructed us, "point it out and I'll cut it down."

We walked and walked down the road in the direction of the sand hills. No trees grew anywhere.

"Can't you see any yet?" Papa asked.

"Ain't no trees here," Ed said.

"Aren't any," I corrected him.

"How about a tumbleweed?" Papa suggested, pulling a spiky round bush from next to the fence where it had tumbled in the wind.

"Looks more like a snowball than a Christmas tree," Ed said.

"What's wrong with that?" Papa asked him.

"It's not tall enough," Frank complained. "It won't touch the ceiling."

"We might hang it up there. Then Howie can't reach to pull the decorations off."

"Look!" I screamed, pointing to a tall, prickly, green plant growing with the tumbleweeds. "It looks almost like a C-C-Christmas tree."

Papa laughed. "I wondered when you'd notice," he said. "Those kosher weeds look just like junipers—perfect for Christmas trees."

"Not bad," Ed conceded.

"We can put it in a bucket of water," Papa said, "to keep it fresh."

"Let's find the biggest one," Ed said, walking along the fence row.

We finally agreed on a "tree" that was tall and full and almost perfectly cone-shaped. Papa cut it off and put it across his shoulder to carry home.

"Now let's get into the spirit of the season," he encouraged.

"How?" Ed wanted to know. "When there's no snow?"

"Let's see if we can think of enough different Christmas carols," Papa challenged, "to last all the way home."

"Silent Night," I suggested.

"Oh Little Town of Bethlehem," Ed offered.

"The one about the wise men following yonder star," Frank said.

"That's a good one to begin with," Papa agreed. "We can pretend we're the three kings traveling afar."

"And one queen," I insisted.

"Yes," Papa laughed, "three wise men and one wise lady."

The air was filled with singing and our hearts were filled with joy as we hiked homeward in the bright desert twilight bearing a prickly weed to decorate for our Christmas tree.

We draped it with popcorn strings and paper chains made from the bright Christmas paper that was wrapped around our purchases from Younger's General Merchandise store. Mama had brought the shiny silver star for the top all the way from Utah.

There weren't many new playthings that first Christmas in New Mexico. Papa had carved a little rolling pin for me, a top for Ed, and something else for each of the other children, and Mama had sewed some new nighties, pajamas, and doll dresses. Santa Claus left a peppermint stick, a handful of nuts, and an orange in each of the stockings.

The most exciting thing about Christmas, though, was something else.

Several times each day Papa had dropped a bucket down the deep well, hoping to hear a splash. The best he could get was damp sand sticking to the bottom. It had happened so often that none of us paid any attention anymore when Papa tried the well for water. But that morning, no matter where we were, we heard him scream and all came running.

"*Eureka*!" he shouted, "*I have found it*! Eureka! Hallelujah! Hosanna and Hooray!"

He pulled the bucket out brimming over with water, set it down on the ground, plunged both arms in, and pulled them out to let the water run off.

"Water," he said quietly, as if the word were sacred. "Water."

Then he looked up toward the sky and whispered, "Thank you, God. Thank you."

I couldn't tell if he'd splashed on his face or if it was tears that made it wet.

"That's the best present we could ever have," Mama said, hugging Papa first and then all the rest of us. She picked up Howie last and whirled him around in a circle.

"Let's celebrate," she said, "with pancakes for breakfast."

"Hurry, then," Papa said. "We have to get the pipe and sucker rods in."

"What are sucker rods?" Ed wanted to know.

"Those long wooden poles leaning against the barn. They suck the water out of the ground."

"Where do you put them?" I asked.

"First we put a big pipe down into the well. Then we put the sucker rods, one at a time, inside that and push them down in the sand as far as they'll go."

"What if they aren't long enough?" Ed asked.

"We'll fasten another onc onto the first. They're made so they can be screwed together."

"Then will the water come up?"

"Yes, and we'll need a windmill to pump it up into the storage tank."

"Why?" I asked.

"So we'll always have plenty of water."

"Where is the tank?"

"I ordered one from the catalog," Papa said. "It should be here in a week or two."

"Did you order a windmill, too?"

"Nope," Papa said, "I'll have to build that."

"Pancakes are ready," Mama announced, "with some of Grandma's good raspberry jam."

"I didn't know we had any of that left," Papa said.

"I've been saving it for Christmas," Mama told him.

"Well, it will serve a double purpose today," Papa said as he bowed his head to give thanks for the food—and especially for the water.

I could hear the pancakes sizzling hotter and hotter in the pan and smelled them burning long before Papa was finished with his prayer. Mama had plenty more batter, though, and before long our stomachs were as full of good food as our hearts were full of excitement.

As soon as the sucker rods were down in the well, Papa got busy making some furniture. He had already hammered together a table and benches so everyone could sit down to eat. He built a small sofa, and Mama made cushions for it so there would be a nice place for company to sit in the daytime and for Caroline to sleep at night.

Next Papa fixed a trundle bed for Frank and Howie that could slide under the big bed when they weren't using it. That was all our one-room house could hold.

On New Year's Day, Mama reminded us that, now Christmas vacation was over, it was time for everyone to get back into school.

"You've missed too much already," she said.

Ed groaned, I grinned, Carolyn shrugged her shoulders, and Frank looked scared.

When I came down from the loft the next morning wearing my second-best dress, Mama could tell that I was expecting to go to school with the others. She shook her head.

"Oh, no, Dora," she pleaded, "not yet."

"I c-can talk!" I insisted.

"Of course you can," she agreed, "but you still stutter some."

"N-not much,"

"You're right. Not much. But the problem with stuttering," she explained, "is that it gets worse and worse if people tease you about it, and if you go to school . . . " She just shook her head as if she knew what would happen there and grabbed me in a hug.

"I know it breaks your heart not to go to school," she whispered in my ear, "but it would break it even more if you got like Cousin Mary, wouldn't it?"

I had forgotten all about Cousin Mary. She stuttered so much that she never had a chance to finish a sentence because no one could stand to listen to her long enough. Someone else always completed it for her.

No, I didn't want to be like that.

"If we work hard right now," Mama went on, "I think we can nip that little problem right in the bud before it gets any worse. Then you can go to school with nothing to worry about."

I nodded, trying to blink fast enough to keep the tears from spilling out.

"I'll get you a set of ABCs," she promised, "and you can study at home. I saw some in Younger's window."

After Mama had gone with the others, I stayed sitting at the breakfast table, staring straight ahead, not wanting to do anything.

"Why the long face, sweetheart?" Papa asked.

"You know," I replied.

"Wish you could go to school, huh?"

I nodded.

"Sure are a lot of advantages, all right, to having an education," he observed.

I nodded again.

"Lots of advantages to staying home, too."

"Like what?" I wanted to know.

"Like getting to help your papa do things."

I asked with my eyes what kind of advantage that was supposed to be. I helped Papa every day, and it was hard work, not play.

"And finding out the secrets," he continued, "before anyone else does. You were the first to know about the move to New Mexico, remember?"

I nodded in agreement.

"Well, maybe there's another secret," he said.

Chapter 16

Another Secret

"Like what?" My enthusiasm was lukewarm.

"Wait and see," Papa said mysteriously. "I promise you'll like it better than school."

"Bet I won't."

"Bet you will."

"Tell me then."

"Just be patient."

"P-p-please, Papa," I coaxed.

He shook his head. "You'll find out soon enough," he promised.

Knowing there was a secret and not knowing what it was was even worse than knowing one and not being able to tell it. I followed Papa everywhere he went, trying to pry it out of him. I couldn't do it. Finally I gave up.

"I need the ABCs," I told Mama the day after school started.

"Yes," Mama agreed, "I'm planning to take you

to Younger's as soon as I finish kneading this bread dough."

When we got to the store, the ABCs were still on display so we hurried inside to buy them. Mr. Younger pulled out a new box and told Mama the price.

"Oh, dear," she said, "I didn't think they'd be that much."

My heart felt heavy. What if we didn't have enough money?

"I could let you have the ones in the window for less," Mr. Younger said. "Some are faded a little, and the box is lost, but all the letters are there."

"That will be fine," Mama said.

"Are they for the little lady here?" the storekeeper asked as he reached for the cards that were spread out in the window. "I know just the thing to put them in so she won't lose any."

He climbed up his ladder, got a flat box down from a high shelf, and brushed it across his pant leg to get rid of the dust. Then he slipped the letters inside and handed it to me. It was a beautiful box with a picture on the lid of an elegant lady in a wide-brimmed hat.

"You can make words till the cows come home," he told me.

That was exactly what I intended to do. I knew right where I was going to hide the box in the barn so no one else would disturb it. Underneath the window ledge between two boards was a space just big enough to stand it on end. I would put my pillow and folded quilt in front and no one would be able to see it.

The first few days I spread the letters on the hay and made words with the cards by looking at the ones I had memorized in the Mother Goose book. I tried to figure out what they said by remembering the rhymes that went with the pictures, but some things just didn't seem to make sense. If W-A-T-E-R spelled "water," why did D-A-U-G-H-T-E-R make "daughter"? The two words sounded almost the same, but they looked so much different. "Nose" and "grows" had the same problem. How come "knife" started with a "k" and "nut" with an "n"?

When I asked Mama about it, she could tell I needed some help and decided to work with me every afternoon while the younger children took naps. She taught me the sounds each letter made and how they fit together to make words. I learned to read "Pat-a-cake" and "This Little Pig."

I studied with the ABCs in the barn loft until my mind got muddled, and then I decided to work on my sampler.

I took the notebook out of my chest and thumbed through the sketches I'd made. I cut around each one and arranged them on the paper with the watermelon pattern around it. I put the slammed door at the beginning, the open door at the end, the maze in the middle, and everything else in the rest of the space.

There was still some room to add some other things that might happen before I got through that schoolroom door. I traced some of the designs onto the cloth and began embroidering again.

Papa got right to work on the windmill, and I was watching him put the finishing touches on the top when he called to me, "Go into the house and get your mama."

When we came out, Papa was hanging upside down from the highest crosspiece. "Look, hon'," he shouted, "it's all finished."

Mama looked up and gasped. "Alfred B. Cookson, you come down here right this minute before *you're* finished. You'll have every last one of these youngsters thinking they can do silly tricks like that up there, and before you know it someone will fall and break his neck."

Papa flipped easily to his feet, climbed down, and ran over to silence her with a kiss. "You worry too much," he said.

"No wonder, with such a crazy husband," she scolded, trying not to smile. "You scared me half to death."

Papa knew she was right about the danger and

used the leftover lumber and pipe to make an acting pole where we could learn to swing upside down and do other tricks at a safe distance from the ground. But when I drew the windmill for my sampler, I put Papa hanging by his heels from the top.

Every Sunday we drove over to Clovis for Sunday School, ate dinner at the Lenstroms', and went to the church meeting in the afternoon. Papa pointed to some galvanized water tanks on the way and said the one he'd ordered for us would be in Texico any day now.

I was outlining the maze in the middle of my sampler with black stitches the day the word came that a freight shipment was waiting to be picked up at the train station. Papa hitched up the horses, and we hurried over to bring it home.

"How can one of those big things fit in our wagon?" I asked.

"Good question," Papa said, and explained that all the pieces came in a box, and we'd have to put them together ourselves.

"How?" I wanted to know.

"Follow the instructions," Papa said.

That didn't look as easy as it sounded when Papa unpacked all the parts and spread them out on the ground. It took the help of all the family, as well as some friends and neighbors, to assemble the tank and put it in place on top of the wooden platform

Papa had built. It had to be up high so the water could run downhill when we needed it.

Before long everything was connected, and the pump run by the windmill was sucking water out of the well and pouring it into the tank. Papa's grin was as wide as a watermelon wedge.

"A farmer always feels better with a water supply," he said.

As Brother Williamson predicted, we had a couple of cold winter storms with a sprinkling of snow, but Papa was always working—clearing off weeds or breaking the ground to plant broom corn in the spring. The cinnamon-colored soil curled away from the plow in light, sandy furrows. Then the harrow laid it out in a soft, level blanket to wait for just the right moment for sowing the seeds.

Papa watched the moon as well as the weather. He insisted that root crops should be planted in the "dark of the moon" and crops that matured above ground when the moon was full.

When Papa saw bare-root fruit trees for sale at the farm-supply store late in January, he decided it was time to get the orchard in.

"Trees need to be planted while they're dormant," he told me.

"What's dormant?" I wanted to know.

"Resting," he explained. "After the leaves have dropped in the fall, it's like the trees go to sleep until a nice warm spring day wakes them up and they burst into bloom and the leaves grow again. They don't even notice if you move them while they're dozing."

I was helping him choose which kinds to buy, and he decided to get two for each of us children.

"You can water them and watch them grow, and when they have fruit you can share it with everyone," he told me.

"I want oranges," I insisted, remembering the wonderful, sweet-but-tangy taste at Christmas.

The clerk shook his head. "It's too cold here for oranges," he told me.

I had to settle for two apples: Early Harvest and Yellow Transparent. Each had a wooden label telling the name, and Papa wrote my name on the tags, too.

As soon as we got home, we planted my two trees and George's and Howie's. Papa put wet gunny sacks around the roots of the others and helped Ed, Caroline, and Frank get theirs in the ground after they got home from school that afternoon.

We had to make sure each one got four buckets of water twice a week, more in hot weather. I helped George water his apple trees, too. They were called June and Alexander.

"June apples are the smallest and the first to get ripe," Papa told him, "and Alexanders are the biggest and make the best pies."

Mama's favorite way to get rid of my stuttering was to have me practice "tongue twisters." She could say some sentences that tied my tongue up in knots: "She sells seashells by the seashore," and "Peter Piper picked a peck of prickly pickled peppers."

"If you can learn to say those words fast enough," she promised, "you'll soon be over that stuttering business."

One day I lay back in the hay, exhausted with the effort of trying to keep my tongue from tangling up. I heard the barn door open and close quietly below and then a soft rustle came from Papa's work room. Whatever he was doing in there, he wasn't making much noise. Maybe it had something to do with the secret. I went down to find out.

Papa was weaving a big oval basket. The sides sloped out a little, and the top was finished with a braided edge that turned into a small handle on each side. It looked pretty fancy for a wash basket.

"Whatcha making?" I asked.

"Basket," he said.

"What for?"

"Mama."

"She know about it?"

He shook his head. "Surprise," he whispered.

So that was the secret. Another basket for Mama. How could that be more exciting than school? Disappointment dragged down on my shoulders and made them sag.

"What for?" I asked, not really caring.

Papa smiled and, calm as anything, said, "The new baby."

"*The new baby*?" I screamed. "Really? Truly?"

"Really, truly," he said. "But I wouldn't scream a secret if I were you."

"How do you know?" I whispered.

"I just know," he whispered back.

"How?" I repeated.

"I just do," he said in his that's-something-too-special-to-talk-about voice.

I decided to try another question. "When?" I asked.

"Pretty soon," he told me. "Isn't that more exciting than school?"

"Oh, yes! Yes! Yes! Yes!" I hugged him so tight that he pulled my arms away from his neck.

"You're choking me!" he gasped, and I let go.

"Boy or girl?" I whispered in his ear.

"Don't know," he told me. "Only God knows that."

"I hope it's a sister," I said. I'd hoped for a sister ever since Elizabeth Ann was born into the Owens family on the way to New Mexico.

"Well, don't hope it out loud," Papa warned me. "Remember, a secret is a secret."

"Does anyone else know?"

"Only Mama."

"I won't tell," I promised.

I was afraid my face would tell. Such happiness as I felt seemed impossible to hide. I imagined it shining from my skin like a warm, glowing halo that matched the feeling I had inside.

Mama noticed the difference. "That's pretty happy humming for a girl who's washing the dishes," she observed.

"Mm-hmm," I answered and kept on humming. I was planning my own surprise. I wanted to make something for the baby, something as soft and cozy and lovely as the secret I was carrying in my heart. Like the doll shawl I had given Ilene.

After I finished the dishes, I went to see what leftover yarn I could find to crochet it with, but there wasn't enough to make anything. I did find some fresh flannel scraps in the rag bag, however. I figured out that Mama had been sewing some new baby clothes while I was busy doing other things.

I decided to cut out some squares and sew them together into a little quilt. I embroidered a yellow daisy in each of the blocks except the center one. In that one I put the initials "I.C." Boy or girl, in our alphabetical family the baby's name would begin with the letter "I."

Maybe the new baby could have the same name

as my friend back in Utah: Ilene. Or Isabel. Or maybe Ina. Such lovely names. I didn't want to think that maybe the baby might have to be an Ira or Isaac or Irving. After four boys in a row, it was time for another girl.

I made the back of the quilt from the bright calico scraps left over from my Sunday dress so the baby would like looking at it. I had to ask Mama for some batting to put in the middle, and she wanted to know what I was making.

"Something for a little doll," I told her.

After I had tied yellow yarn bows through the corners of each block and finished the edges of the quilt, I held it up to my cheek to try out the softness and then tucked it in the basket in the barn and waited for the baby to be born.

Waiting for a secret to happen is even worse than all the knowing, not knowing, or not telling. The days seemed to get longer and longer, like taffy stretched between the fingers.

I could tell that Mama was getting anxious, too. I still had all those questions that I wanted to ask her about how babies got here from heaven, but I had promised Papa I wouldn't talk about the secret, so I saved them for later.

On Valentine's Day I was helping George and Howie cut out some red paper hearts when Mama said, "Sister Lenstrom's invited you and the boys over to make some cookies."

"Goody!" I said, jumping up from the table.

"If I let you go, can you watch George and Howard so they won't be any bother?"

All of a sudden, *Howie* had become *Howard*. Mama had been referring to him as "my little man" a lot lately and telling him how big he was growing. It seemed to me that it should be clear to everyone that he wasn't going to be the baby of the family much longer. But if anyone else had guessed the secret, they didn't let on.

I was eager for any break in the monotony of waiting and wondering when it would happen, so a morning in the sweet-smelling Lenstrom kitchen was as tempting as a carrot to a pony.

"Will I be able to stay until Jenny gets home from school so we can play house?" I asked.

"Maybe," Mama told me. "Depends on when Papa can come to get you."

I took Henrietta, just in case. The Lenstrom girls had all sorts of child-size furniture that their daddy had made and a regular little playhouse in a corner of their kitchen.

Mama helped to settle the boys in the wagon and waved as we drove away. Papa was as jolly as a jaybird, singing and hurrying the horses along as if we were nearly late for a picnic. When we got to our friends' house, he jumped down from the wagon seat, lifted the boys out, said a few words to Sister Lenstrom, and was gone.

It seemed like no time at all until he was back again. Dozens of warm cookies were spread out on brown paper all ready to eat when the girls came home from school. I had set the small table for a play dinner, and Sister Lenstrom poured milk in the toy cups. Papa called to me as he drove up in front of the house, and I went out to the wagon.

"I don't want to go home yet," I told him.

"Not even to see the Valentine surprise?" he asked.

Chapter 17

The Singing Spring

"Is the baby born already?" I wanted to know.

"Yup," Papa told me, "about one o'clock."

"Is it a . . ."

"Girl? Yes, a little angel with dimples and yellow hair, just like yours. We decided to name her Irene because that means *peace*. With such a big family we need a peaceful baby."

Irene. Almost the same as *Ilene*, but not exactly. Irene. That was more beautiful than any of the names I'd thought of. And imagine, a little girl who looked like me. It seemed too good to be true. What do you say when a secret turns out even better than you'd ever imagined? I couldn't think of a thing.

"Well, don't just stand there with your mouth open," Papa said. "Go tell everybody about it!"

So I did. I was so excited that I stuttered a little, but I was able to make the Lenstroms understand that we had a new baby sister.

It seemed like the ride home was lots longer than usual because I was so anxious to see the baby. Finally we got there, and I flew into the house to find Mama in bed with a soft little bundle curled in one arm. She was wrapped in the quilt I'd made.

Irene! She was just as pretty and small as a baby doll. Mama let me hold her, and when I touched that angel-soft hair all thoughts of wishing to be in school flew out of my head just like Ed's feathers. I was perfectly content to be at home.

The new basket for the baby didn't fit anywhere. Sometimes it sat on the couch, sometimes on the floor, and sometimes on the dinner table. All day long it was shifted from one place to another to get it out of the way of what was going on.

One day when Papa was moving it again for the fourth or fifth time he said, "I'd better add on a room. We're bursting at the seams."

As usual, when he thought of a project, he was ready to get on with it. In no time at all he had another room built next to the one the family lived in and was ready to cut out the door between them. Now the house was twice as big. It seemed like a palace with a kitchen *and* a bedroom where the baby could sleep without being disturbed. Everyone enjoyed the extra room, but Ed, George, and I were still happy to have our beds in the barn loft.

Just about all Mama had time to do was feed

people. She would no sooner finish nursing the baby than it was time to cook another meal. Then the baby was hungry again. She'd bake the bread, feed the baby, fix dinner, feed the baby, put the supper on, feed the baby. And while the rest of us slept, she'd feed the baby two or three times during the night.

"It's a good thing you didn't go to school this year," Mama told me, "because I need you to be my right-hand helper."

I was so happy to have a baby in the house that I sang all spring. I sang as I swished Irene's clothes clean in the sudsy water. I sang as I hung them out to dry. I sang soothing lullabies when I rocked her to sleep at bedtime. I sang lively nursery rhymes when I tickled her toes and clapped her hands together when she was awake.

I found out that when I sang I didn't stutter. Something about the way the words fit into the tune didn't leave room for any extra sounds, and when there was no room, I didn't say them. I still stuttered some on words that weren't set to a melody, however. So I said the tongue twisters over and over.

We all got busier and busier. Papa was so tired by Saturday night that he didn't even want to think about driving clear over to Clovis for church the next day.

"The horses need a day of rest as much as we

do," he insisted. "Why don't we have Sunday School here at home?"

So we did.

Every minute Papa could spare from working in the fields he spent fixing up the house. First, he dug out a basement so there would be a place to store the bottled fruit and coal for the stove. In one corner he made a root cellar to keep carrots, potatoes, and parsnips after they were dug in the fall. On top of the basement, he built a front room and a porch, making the house face a different direction than before so the water tank was at the side instead of in front.

One warm March day I carried baby Irene outside in her basket so she could kick in the sunshine while I spaded up a spot for my own garden near the house. I was still digging when Papa came in from the field for dinner.

"What are you going to plant?" he asked.

"Beans, watermelon, and maple trees," I told him.

"Maple trees?" he said. "We'll never find maple trees in this state."

"Don't worry," I said, "I brought the seeds with me."

"What a good idea!" Papa exclaimed. "I hope they grow. This place could sure use some trees."

"I brought my other seeds, too."

"Clear from Utah," he marveled. "That makes

them pretty special. We wouldn't want anything to happen to them. I'll help you build a fence around your plot to keep out the animals."

I had no idea how much work a big garden was going to be when I helped Mama plant hers. She had every kind of vegetable seed she could beg, borrow, or buy. We sowed row after row of beans, beets, turnips, carrots, sweet corn, spinach, chard, squash, tomatoes, potatoes, parsnips, and cucumbers. And a great big watermelon patch.

As soon as the shoots were out of the ground, we had to start on the weeding, watering, and thinning. That was only the beginning.

None of my maple wings grew, and a crow got the beans. But all six watermelon seeds sprouted, and I tended them like babies.

Just before school was out, Mama borrowed some first-grade books from the teacher to keep over the summer so I could learn to read. I could sound out most of the words, and she helped me with the rest.

Reading books was the most fun I had ever had. To think that all those letters on a page could tell a story I'd never heard or explain something I didn't know! It seemed like some kind of magic miracle. I read them again and again until I had them all memorized.

The broom corn was growing in straight green rows. We had weeded out the weaker plants and stripped off the suckers, and the remaining stalks were as high as my head. Papa had a job in mind that I'd never heard of before. One day he pulled three white crayons out of his pocket and handed them to Caroline, Ed, and me.

"I want you to draw a line around the bottom of each cornstalk," he instructed, "to keep the ants from crawling up." He showed us what he meant. "They won't cross that greasy line," he explained.

"Will ants hurt the c-corn?" I wanted to know.

"No, but the aphids will," Papa told us, "and where there are ants there are aphids."

"Why?"

"The ants move them from one place to another to be their 'cows.' The aphids suck up the plant juices and make a sweet fluid called honeydew, which the ants 'milk' and lick off their backs. One little aphid can't do much damage by itself, but they multiply so fast that, before you turn around twice, the whole plant is covered, and soon all its strength is sucked away. We can't afford to lose our corn. It's our only cash crop."

"Do we have to do all of it?" Caroline asked.

"Every plant," Papa said. "If you do three rows a day, it will soon be done."

"Three rows!" Ed complained. "That's impossible!"

"Okay, two then," Papa compromised, "to start with. Now get to work."

I looked at the corn patch. All I could see was a solid green wall. But I knew how long the rows stretched out behind it because I had walked along them with Papa while he planted the seeds. Each one went farther away than down the long lane from our place to Grandma's back home in Utah. There were thousands of sturdy stalks to circle with white crayons—maybe even millions.

"It will take us forever," Caroline worried. She helped mostly in the house and wasn't used to outside work.

"Oh, no, not forever," Papa promised. "Only a week or two."

The first day seemed like forever. It was horrible. Our backs were killing us long before we were done. The rows seemed to go on for miles, and no one finished even two. We were so tired at the end of the day that we could hardly force ourselves to walk to the house, and we fell into bed the minute supper was over.

The next day was worse. When we tried to figure out where to start, we couldn't tell which plants we'd already done because the heat had melted the crayon marks and they were invisible.

"All that work and you can't even tell we did it," Ed grumbled.

"I hope Papa can," Caroline said.

"I hope the ants can," I added.

Our backs never quit aching. The third day was even worse than the first two.

Just when I thought I could never live through another day of bending over and circling cornstalks, the pain began to ease. It seemed that if I kept forcing my muscles to do more than they wanted to, they finally quit complaining and became stronger than ever. The lesson I learned came in handy later.

By the time the job was finished, I had worked out a rhythm that made the work easy and efficient. Standing between two rows with a crayon in each hand, I reached out in both directions to circle two stalks at once, then moved backwards to the next pair.

I imagined my hands were dancing the same step over and over—a loop and a line, a loop and a line. I planned to embroider that double-track design on my sampler.

While I worked, I sang the tongue twister I'd made up so I could get rid of my stutter while I worked. I repeated, "Crayons circle cornstalks," faster and faster as I speeded up my movements to keep up with the tempo. I soon got ahead of both Ed and Caroline, and on the last day I helped them finish their rows.

I watched as more and more grey-green scalloped

leaves grew on my watermelon vines and two different kinds of yellow blossoms opened out. One kind had a green blob under it that would grow into a melon if the bees carried some golden grains of pollen from the center of the other kind.

"Just in case the bees are busy somewhere else," Mama said, "you can pollinate with your finger." She showed me how.

No matter how long the sunny summer days stretched out, there weren't enough hours to finish all the work. Once the garden started to produce, there was no way to turn it off. Mama was determined not to waste a bit of it. What we couldn't eat, we put away for winter. We bottled, pickled, and dried vegetables until I didn't want to see the next day begin.

When the neighbors told Papa that they had extra fruit in their orchards, he sent us to pick it, and we bottled that, too.

One Saturday in July I went to town with Mama to buy some more fruit jars, and we met Lucy and Sister Williamson right in front of the hardware store.

"Why, Betty Cookson," Lucy's mother said, "I haven't seen you for a month of Sundays. Hope no one's been sick so you couldn't come out to church."

"No, we're fine," Mama assured her. "Alfred's been working the horses pretty hard, and he says they need a day of rest on Sunday even more than we do. When we can get another team he'll trade off, and then we can drive into Clovis for church."

"Is that all? Why don't we just stop by and pick you up, then?"

"Oh, no, that's too much trouble."

"No trouble at all. Lucy'll be glad for a friend to go to Sunday School with. Our wagon's plenty big."

I really wanted to go to church again. As much as anything I was anxious to get away from the never-ending summer work. Cucumbers grew on Sundays the same as any other days and had to be picked and pickled.

"P-Please, Mama," I coaxed.

"Maybe the girls could go," Mama said. "The boys don't have any shoes right now. We couldn't afford both fruit trees and shoes, and we needed to get the orchard in this year."

That was the first I knew that we were getting short of money. No wonder we had to bottle all the food we could while it was growing in the garden. And the *real* reason we missed church so much must be because the boys had worn out their shoes.

"That's right," Sister Williamson agreed with Mama. "First things first. We'll stop by for Caroline and Dora, then. About nine in the morning."

"We'd be very grateful," Mama said.

When I tried on my only Sunday dress that night, it was too short.

"You're growing like a weed," Mama said. "I need to sew a piece on the bottom."

I reminded her that I'd used the cloth that matched my dress for the back of Irene's quilt, so Mama tacked on a ruffle cut out of the only material she could find—a printed flour sack.

Caroline's Sunday shoes pinched her toes, but she didn't tell Mama because she was as eager as I was to get dressed up and go somewhere.

We were ready and waiting long before the Williamsons drove into the yard to pick us up the next morning. I was so happy to be going to church that I hugged my Bible and sang hymns all the way to the meetinghouse. I felt so good that I shouldn't have been surprised to find out that something bad was bound to happen.

Chapter 18

The Other Side

As before, it was the Brownly boys who caused the trouble. I saw them as soon as I climbed down out of the wagon in Clovis.

"Well, well," Bradford said, "look what the cat dragged in."

"Yeah," Benjamin agreed.

"So some of the Cooksons finally decided to come to church, did they?" Brad continued.

"Finally," Ben echoed.

"Where's Ed?" Bradford asked.

"Yeah, where's Ed?"

"Home," Caroline said.

"How come?"

"He's busy." Caroline didn't want to say he didn't have any shoes.

"Workin' on Sunday?" Bradford asked.

"Breakin' the Sabbath?" Ben accused.

"No, not breaking the Sabbath," Caroline replied

in an icy tone of voice that made Bradford decide to change the subject.

"Did Dumb Dora ever learn to talk yet?" he asked Caroline as if I were not even there.

"Yeah, can she talk yet?"

I was so insulted and angry that I shouted the answer myself, "Of c-c-c-course I c-c-c-can!"

I couldn't believe how the words came out. I had never stuttered like that before. I hadn't worried about my talking for a long time. I just did it. All my family was used to the way I said things and had no trouble understanding me. I thought I had stopped stuttering completely and was looking forward to starting school in September.

Now I found out that, the minute I got nervous, the words trembled on the end of my tongue as if I were shivering with a chill. My face burned as hot as fire, and Bradford decided to fan the flame.

"Of c-c-c-course you c-c-c-can," he laughed.

"Of c-c-c-c-course!" Benjamin repeated.

"D-d-d-d-dumb D-D-D-D-Dora," Bradford teased, and his brother doubled my embarrassment with his echo, "D-dumb-dumb-dumb D-Dora-Dora-Dora."

I tried to blink back the tears, but they poured out anyway. Caroline put an arm around me from one side and Lucy from the other, and they led me to a seat inside the building. The day was ruined. My life was ruined.

I sat in miserable silence until the meeting was over; then I hurried to the Williamsons' wagon, climbed in, hunkered down, and tried to become invisible. I didn't feel like singing on the way home.

When we got there, I told Mama that I was never going to go to church again.

"Me neither," Caroline announced, kicking off her shoes. "My feet are killing me!"

"Or s-school either," I sobbed. When I said that, Mama could tell that something really dreadful had happened and sat down with us to hear the whole story. Caroline repeated what Bradford and Benjamin had said, and Mama became more and more angry with every word until she was furious.

She started out the door all ready to hitch up the horses and drive over to Brownlys' and give them a piece of her mind about what the boys had done to me.

Papa held out an arm to stop her. "Calm down," he told her. "That'd do more harm than good. If you'll just put a big pot of water on the stove, Dora and I will go out to the garden to see if we can find some corn for dinner."

Papa knew that walking down the whispering rows of sweet corn hunting for ears that were ripe enough to eat would make me feel better. No vegetable is so deliciously sweet as fresh corn on the cob popped into boiling water as soon as it is picked.

If a cob felt full and hard and the silk was frizzled brown on top, it was ready, and Papa grabbed it firmly and cracked it off with a quick downward jerk.

Sometimes there were little baby ears growing next to the big ears. The small ones had long pink or green silky hair as smooth and shiny as satin. I saved those little corn dolls to play house with.

"Look," Papa said as he pulled the husks off a particularly fat cob, "here're twins." He handed them to me.

The I-hate-the-Brownly-boys frown that had been frozen on my face melted into a smile. I brushed the soft silk against my cheek and wiped away the tears.

"That's my girl," Papa said. "Now keep a smile on your face and don't let any mean boys decide whether you go to school or not. That's just a lesson to learn from, not the end of the world. Any girl that can draw around as many cornstalks as you did is certainly tough enough to lick a little problem like stuttering once in a while."

He was right. I could do it. That corn job had taught me that if I kept on pushing when things were hard, they got easier.

"Those Brownlys live too far away to go to our school anyway," Papa reminded me. "Now, let's go find a nice, sweet watermelon to go with the corn."

Watermelon was the best thing about the farm. I loved the crisp, cracking sound when the knife bit into the green shell and spread open the luscious fruit, colored like a rosebud and speckled with flat and shiny black seeds, just right for spitting target practice. My face was always sticky from being buried in a piece.

Best of all, no one had to bottle, dry, pickle, or preserve melons. They were just for enjoying while they were fresh, juicy, and yummy sweet. I'd heard of watermelon-rind preserves and was afraid Mama would decide to make and bottle some. But she didn't.

"Summer'll be gone before we know it," Papa said one day. "I see that they're cleaning up the school grounds and even painting the building. That new teacher must be a real go-getter."

"His name would choke a horse," Mama complained. "It's bad enough to tie Dora's tongue in knots."

"W-What's his name?" I asked.

"McLaughlin," she said. "Mr. McLaughlin."

She was right. I would never be able to say it. "M" was the worst letter to stutter on. It could make my lips chatter like a case of the shivers. The other part of the name was like stirring a mouthful of mush with my tongue.

But having a problem is one thing and doing something about it is another. It was time I got on with a solution.

When I passed the scarecrow hanging on a fence-post by the cornfield I had an idea. I looked at it and pretended it was the schoolteacher.

"Good m-m-morning, M-M-Mr. M-M-McLaughlin," I said. I'd have to practice a lot to get rid of all the extra "M's" that trembled on my lips when I said that name. I knew that if I stuttered on it, Mama would keep me home from school again. I was determined to be on the other side of that door this year.

I spent hours and hours in front of the scarecrow, practicing the teacher's name over and over again. I still stammered once in a while, so I began to sing the words to a made-up tune. That worked just fine. I decided that everytime I said "Mr. McLaughlin" I could pretend I was singing it.

August moved right along toward my tenth birthday on the twenty-ninth. Soon school would be starting again. Could I convince Mama that I was ready to go?

I didn't expect the answer to my question to be wrapped up in a box and handed to me for a present, but it was. Inside were a blue calico dress and a pair of new shoes. The only possible thing I could need them for was school.

I didn't know how to act when the dream of my life was about to come true. I had always thought I would climb up on the windmill, wave my arms around with the blades, and shout, "Hooray!"

I could picture my voice flying around in the whir and spinning off with the breeze to carry my excitement in echoes out into the air for all the world to hear. "I'm going to school . . . going to school . . . to school . . . school . . . "

Instead it seemed that my voice was closed off by a hard lump that felt as if my heart had jumped up in my throat. A silly tear trickled down my cheek, and my chin shivered.

"Hey," Papa said, "it's nothing to cry about. I thought you wanted to go to school."

"I do," I whispered. "Oh, I do."

"Then smile about it," Mama suggested. I lifted the corners of my trembling lips.

Later in the day I walked by myself over to the schoolhouse and looked at the newly painted door that would soon be open to me. I imagined all the wonders inside: books and maps and pictures of faraway places. Numbers written above or below each other, or side by side, that solved problems about how many apples or how much butter. Make-believe tales about fairies and princesses and little green elves. True stories about heroes and heroines and black-hearted pirates. History books telling about things that happened in the past to famous people. Poems to memorize. Experiments about how things worked. There would be thousands of things to arrange on the shelves of my mind and new friends to play with and talk to. It all seemed too good to be true.

As I walked slowly home, I practiced my greeting to the teacher, "Good morning, Mr. McLaughlin."

In the days that followed, I addressed the scarecrow as Mr. McLaughlin over and over. I repeated the nursery rhymes to Irene, recited the first-grade books to Howard, and tried out all the sounds of the alphabet letters.

While I practiced the tongue twisters, I finished the embroidery on my sampler. The open door was all stitched, painted white. When the time came to go through it, I was ready. Whatever combination of good things and bad ones lay ahead, I was prepared to face them.

On the first day of school, I walked over with Ed, Caroline, and Frank as I had done many times before. After the bell rang, I stayed in the play yard and watched everyone else file into the building, as usual. Then I looked down to make sure my shoelaces were tied, smoothed my new blue calico dress, took a deep breath, and walked eagerly up the steps and through the entrance.

"Good morning, Mr. McLaughlin," I said. The words came out as clear as crystal. "My name is Dora Cookson, and I'm going to be in your class this year."

I smiled until I could feel my dimples sink into

deep holes. Oh, it is wonderful to know the good news and to be able to tell it!

I reached behind me for the knob and quietly pulled the heavy wooden slab closed behind me. I was on the other side of the schoolroom door at last!

About the Author

"I call myself a full-time nothing and a part-time everything," says Joy Hulme. Besides her writing, she enjoys creating stained glass and arranging flowers for weddings and funerals. (She even grows some of the flowers herself.)

Joy has published many articles, short stories, and other writings, including *A Stable in Bethlehem,* a Little Golden Christmas Book. "My mother was a writer," she says, "and she encouraged me. I had a little desk outside, behind the garage. It was in the woods, really—we lived on a ten-acre plot in the Cottonwood area south of Salt Lake City, Utah. I used to go out there to write my ideas."

The idea for *The Other Side of the Door* came from a woman Joy used to visit regularly. The book is based on this woman's true experiences. Joy even found the deed to the family's original homestead in New Mexico when she visited there one summer.

Joy and her husband, Melvin, have been married for forty-six years. They have five children and twenty-one grandchildren and live in Monte Sereno, California.

Look for These Books from Cinnamon Tree

The Lucky Series: *Lucky's Crash Landing, Lucky Breaks Loose,* and ***Lucky's Gold Mine,*** by Dean Hughes
Is Lucky really lucky? He gets into more accidents than anyone you'll ever meet. Sidewalk cracks reach out and grab his shoes. Steps suddenly disappear under his feet. His father is in a business that checks out disasters, so they travel from place to place in their motorhome. Ron Ladd, Lucky's father, insists that no one is luckier. The worst accidents don't seem to affect Lucky much. In *Lucky's Crash Landing,* Lucky tries out skateboarding. In *Lucky Breaks Loose,* he joins a football team. And in *Lucky's Gold Mine,* he searches for lost riches. Get Lucky with all three novels.

Enchantress of Crumbledown, by Donald R. Marshall
Ashley, Brittany, and Tiger run away from their foster home to survive on their own in an abandoned cottage in the woods. Then they discover that they're not alone. An eccentric old woman, Cassandra du Maurier, lives in the cottage too. The four of them embark on a fantastic adventure that ends when the police discover them. Find out what life can really be like when you have someone like Cassandra with you.

The Lord Needed a Prophet, by Susan Arrington Madsen.
Which president of the Church once played a high school basketball game in a drained swimming pool? Which prophet had a job sewing buttons on overalls for ZCMI? Modern-day prophets were once young too—playing, riding horses, and chasing girls with caterpillars. You'll enjoy reading about their families, their missions, their testimonies, their hobbies and interests, and their accomplishments.

A Lasting Peace, by Carol Lynn Pearson
It's 1856, and war is breaking out between the settlers and the Ute Indians in Utah Valley. Then twelve-year-old Sol McAllister saves the life of the Ute chief, Arrowpine. To his surprise, he finds himself in the dangerous position of being the last person who can stop the upcoming rampage. What can a twelve-year-old do to bring about a lasting peace?